The Journal of the Learning Sciences

Volume 6, Number 1   1997

SPECIAL ISSUE:
CONCEPTUAL CHANGE
Ashwin Ram, Nancy J. Nersessian, and Frank C. Keil
Guest Editors

SUBSCRIBER INFORMATION

The Journal of the Learning Sciences is published four times a year and is available on a calendar-year basis only. In the United States and Canada, per-volume rates are U.S. $39.00 for individuals and U.S. $185 for institutions; in other countries, per-volume rates are U.S. $69.00 for individuals and U.S. $215 for institutions. Send subscription orders, information requests, and address changes to the Journal Subscription Department, Lawrence Erlbaum Associates, Inc., 10 Industrial Avenue, Mahwah, NJ 07430–2262. Address changes should include the mailing label or a facsimile. Claims for missing issues cannot be honored beyond 4 months after mailing date. Duplicate copies cannot be sent to replace issues not delivered due to failure to notify publisher of change of address.

This journal is abstracted or indexed in *Contents Pages in Education; ISI: Current Contents/Social & Behavioral Sciences, Social Sciences Citation Index, Research Alert, Social SciSearch; Linguistics and Language Behavior Abstracts; PsycINFO/Psychological Abstracts;* and *Sociological Abstracts.*

Microform copies of this journal are available through UMI, Periodical Check-In, North Zeeb Road, P. O. Box 1346, Ann Arbor, MI 48106–1346.

THE JOURNAL OF THE LEARNING SCIENCES, 6(1), 1–2

[handwritten: title to indicate nothing on social science]

Guest Editors' Introduction

Ashwin Ram and Nancy J. Nersessian

Cognitive Science Program
Georgia Institute of Technology

Frank C. Keil

Department of Psychology
Cornell University

Conceptual change continues to be a central concern of many of the disciplines that participate in the learning sciences. In this issue of *The Journal of the Learning Sciences,* as in the field, the topic is studied from a variety of perspectives. Cognitive development has been concerned with the nature of children's concepts, how they relate to adult concepts, and how they change over the developmental process. Philosophical and historical research on scientific conceptual change has investigated how new conceptual structures are constructed in a scientific community and come to replace existing ones and has discussed the implications of conceptual change for understanding the nature and development of scientific knowledge. Research in science learning has been concerned with the nature of students' intuitive concepts and the role they play in impeding or facilitating learning a science and with developing pedagogical strategies to facilitate the change from intuitive to scientific understanding. Artificial intelligence researchers have been creating computational models of conceptual and representational change. In all of these fields, there is considerable debate as to what constitutes conceptual change and how significant it is to understanding development, science, and learning.

This special issue brings together a variety of perspectives and approaches addressing common fundamental problems of conceptual change: What it is, how it occurs, and how to facilitate it. To represent these perspectives, we used an interdisciplinary team of cognitive scientists as editors—a computer scientist specializing in artificial intelligence (Ashwin Ram), a philosopher and historian of science (Nancy Nersessian), and a developmental psychologist (Frank Keil)—and

Requests for reprints should be sent to Ashwin Ram, College of Computing, Georgia Institute of Technology, Atlanta, GA 30332–0280. E-mail: ashwin@cc.gatech.edu the editorial board and reviewers of this journal who specialize in learning and education. Seventeen articles were received in response to our call, of which four were selected and revised through a rigorous peer review process and printed in this issue.

The issue starts with an article that articulates the role of analogy in conceptual change. In this article, Gentner, Brem, Ferguson, Markman, Levidow, Wolff, and Forbus propose four mechanisms by which analogy can bring about changes in knowledge and discuss whether these mechanisms can change concepts as well as the theoretical structures that relate these concepts. Gentner and her colleagues begin with a historical study of the works of Johannes Kepler. They establish that Kepler used analogy extensively; in fact, Kepler himself discusses this in his writings. They show that analogy was central in bringing about the conceptual change in Kepler's understanding of astronomical phenomena, and they propose a computational model of the four mechanisms of analogy that may explain how Kepler developed his theory of planetary motion.

In the second article, Solomon provides an interesting and very different perspective on conceptual change. He discusses his research into the acquisition of wine expertise and points out that this domain involves both strong perceptual and cognitive components. Because of this, conceptual change in this domain requires not only a move from a perceptually driven to a conceptually driven recognition of the salient features that characterize the concepts but also a restructuring of the system of classification that is the basis for assessing the similarity of concepts.

The third article, by Zietsman and Clement, focuses on conceptual change in science learning in a school setting. They show that extreme cases play a pivotal role in the deep understanding and learning processes that result in conceptual change. Specifically, they argue that extreme cases aid in the construction of explanatory models of scientific phenomena by activating perceptual motor schemas and by facilitating the formation of causal relations between concepts. Extreme cases have been proposed as an important element in understanding expert problem solving; it is interesting that Zietsman and Clement's research shows that extreme cases should play an important role in science education in the schools as well.

The issue closes with Magnusson, Templin, and Boyle's article on conceptual development in which they propose a method of assessing learning that can be used to study the processes (and not just the outcome) of knowledge construction. This allows them to investigate how students use existing knowledge to construct new scientific concepts. Conceptual change, in their view, can be cast as a constructivist process of developing new knowledge through complex problem solving and physical interaction with the phenomena of interest.

Together, these articles provide valuable insights into psychological, philosophical, educational, and computational issues in the study of conceptual change and discuss the implications of the analyses for understanding the fundamental nature and processes of conceptual change.

THE JOURNAL OF THE LEARNING SCIENCES, 6(1), 3–40

Analogical Reasoning and Conceptual Change: A Case Study of Johannes Kepler

Dedre Gentner and Sarah Brem
Department of Psychology
Northwestern University

Ronald W. Ferguson
Department of Computer Science
Northwestern University

Arthur B. Markman
Department of Psychology
Columbia University

Björn B. Levidow
Connect Soft, Inc.
Seattle, Washington

Phillip Wolff
Department of Psychology
Northwestern University

Kenneth D. Forbus
Department of Computer Science
Northwestern University

The work of Johannes Kepler offers clear examples of conceptual change. In this article, using Kepler's work as a case study, we argue that analogical reasoning

Requests for reprints should be sent to Dedre Gentner, Department of Psychology, Northwestern University, 2029 Sheridan Road, Evanston, IL 60208–2710.

facilitates change of knowledge in four ways: (a) highlighting, (b) projection, (c) rerepresentation, and (d) restructuring. We present these four mechanisms within the context of structure-mapping theory and its computational implementation, the structure-mapping engine. We exemplify these mechanisms using the extended analogies Kepler used in developing a causal theory of planetary motion.

> The roads by which men arrive at their insights into celestial matters seem to me almost as worthy of wonder as those matters in themselves.
> —Johannes Kepler (as cited in Koestler, 1963, p. 261)

Analogy is an important mechanism of change of knowledge. Researchers studying transfer of learning have shown that analogies to prior knowledge can foster insight into new material (Bassok, 1990; Bassok & Holyoak, 1989; Catrambone & Holyoak, 1989; Dunbar, 1994; Forbus, Gentner, & Law, 1995; Gentner & Gentner, 1983; Gentner, Rattermann, & Forbus, 1993; Gick & Holyoak, 1980, 1983; Holyoak, Junn, & Billman, 1984; Holyoak & Thagard, 1989; Keane, 1988; Novick & Holyoak, 1991; Novick & Tversky, 1987; Ross, 1987; Spellman & Holyoak, 1993). These laboratory results are supported by direct and indirect observations of the scientific process. The journals of Boyle, Carnot, Darwin, Faraday, and Maxwell (and Kepler) contain many examples of generative uses of analogy (Darden, 1992; Gentner, 1982; Gentner & Jeziorski, 1993; Nersessian, 1985, 1986, 1992; Nersessian & Resnick, 1989; Ranney & Thagard, 1988; Thagard, 1989; Tweney, 1991; Wiser, 1986; Wiser & Carey, 1983). Modern scientists like Oppenheimer (1956) and Glashow (1980) have commented explicitly on the usefulness of analogy in their work. Nersessian's (1992) detailed analyses of the analogies used by Faraday and Maxwell provide evidence that analogy was useful in the development of electromagnetic field theory. Finally, direct field observations of molecular biologists at work demonstrate that analogy is frequently used in the everyday practice of science (Dunbar, 1994).

Our goal in this article is to show how analogy promotes conceptual change. We first lay out four theoretically driven specific mechanisms by which analogy can act to create changes in knowledge and consider the sorts of changes these processes can bring about. In particular, we ask whether analogical mechanisms can bring about changes in concepts as well as changes in the theoretical structure relating the concepts.

We draw on the works of Kepler (1571–1630) to illustrate our points. The goal of modeling the thought processes of a mind like Kepler's is daunting, to say the least. We make no claim to have captured anything close to Kepler's full cognitive processes. Yet, we consider Kepler a particularly apt subject for the study of analogy and conceptual change. First, his work spanned and contributed to a period of immense change in theory. He inherited from Copernicus a conception of the solar system in which the planets moved in perfect circles at uniform speed. By the end of his career, he had abandoned this simple and beautiful view for a model in which the planets travel in elliptical paths at nonuniform speed, with the Sun as the cause of their motion. Second, Kepler was a prolific analogizer. In his books, journals, and letters he constantly used analogies, some only fleetingly and others with tenacious persistence. In some cases, he returned to an analogy repeatedly across different works, extending and analyzing it further on successive bouts. Third, Kepler's writings are unusually rich in descriptions of his thought processes, including fulsome descriptions of his blind alleys and mistakes. The candor and detail of Kepler's writings helps to mitigate the problems inherent in inferring thought processes after the fact from written records. At least part of Kepler's inclusiveness seems to have stemmed from a fascination with the mental paths that led to his conceptual shifts, as evidenced by the quote at the beginning of this article.

In this article, we trace Kepler's extended analogy between light and the *vis motrix* (a precursor of gravity) and also his further analogy between magnetism and the *vis motrix*. Our goal is to characterize the processes by which these analogies led to changes of knowledge, using structure-mapping theory as a framework. We first describe the basic theory. Then we discuss four mechanisms by which analogy brings about change of beliefs. Finally, we apply this framework to Kepler's analogies.

STRUCTURE-MAPPING THEORY

Structure-mapping theory (SMT; Gentner, 1983, 1989) is based on the assumption that analogy involves a process of alignment and projection. Assertions in a base (or source) domain are placed into correspondence with assertions in a target domain, and further assertions true of the base domain are then inferred to be potentially true of the target. For example, when (as we later discuss) Kepler compared the target domain of the Sun and planet to the base domain of two lodestones, he inferred that if the Sun and planet also have polarity, they may alternately attract and repel one another, depending on whether their "friendly" or "unfriendly" poles are proximate. This illustrates the power of an analogy to provide a whole system of inferences about a novel domain. But a mechanism for inferring new knowledge must be constrained. To be cognitively plausible, a theory of analogical mapping must provide some natural limit to what will be inferred based on the mapping. It must also explain the fact that some analogies and some interpretations of a given analogy are preferred over others, even when no differences in factual accuracy are at stake.

SMT (Gentner, 1983, 1989) and its computational counterpart, the structure-mapping engine (SME; Falkenhainer, Forbus, & Gentner, 1989) meet this need by making strong assumptions about the nature of cognitive representation and how it is used in the mapping process. Structure mapping assumes that domain knowledge is in the form of symbolic structural descriptions that include objects, relations between objects, and higher order relations among whole propositions. On this view, the analogical process is one of structural alignment between two mental representations to find the maximal structurally consistent match between them. A *structurally consistent* match is one that satisfies the constraints of *parallel connectivity* and *one-to-one mapping* (Falkenhainer et al., 1989; Gentner, 1983, 1989; Gentner & Markman, 1993, in press; Halford, 1993; Holyoak & Thagard, 1989; Keane, 1988; Markman & Gentner, 1993a, 1993b; Medin, Goldstone, & Gentner, 1993). *Parallel connectivity* says that if two predicates are matched then their arguments must also match. For example, if the predicate HEAVIER(a,b) matches the predicate HEAVIER(x,y) then a must match x and b must match y. *One-to-one mapping* requires that each element in one representation corresponds to at most one element in the other representation.

To explain why some analogies are better than others, structure mapping uses the principle of systematicity: a preference for mappings that are highly interconnected and contain deep chains of higher order relations (Forbus & Gentner, 1989; Forbus et al., 1995; Gentner, 1983, 1989; Gentner et al., 1993). Thus, the probability that an individual match will be included in the final interpretation of a comparison is greater if it is connected by higher order relations to a common system of predicates (Bowdle & Gentner, 1996; Clement & Gentner, 1991; Gentner & Bowdle, 1994). We focus on two predictions that derive from this framework. First, the correspondences mandated by a comparison are governed not only by local similarity but also by the degree to which the elements play the same roles in the common higher order structure (e.g., Clement & Gentner, 1991; Gentner, 1988; Gentner & Clement, 1988; Spellman & Holyoak, 1993). Relational commonalities thus tend to outweigh object commonalities in determining the interpretation of a comparison. Second, because comparison promotes a structural alignment, differences relevant to the common structure are also highlighted by a comparison (Gentner & Markman, 1994; Markman & Gentner, 1993a, 1993b, 1996, in press). Thus, paradoxically, comparisons can illuminate differences as well as commonalities.

SME simulates the comparison process (Falkenhainer et al., 1989; Falkenhainer, Forbus, & Gentner, 1986). To capture the necessary structural distinctions we use an nth-order typed predicate calculus. Entities stand for the objects or reified concepts in the domain (e.g., planet, orbit). Attributes are unary predicates used to describe independent descriptive properties of objects (e.g., HEAVY(planet)). Functions[1] are used primarily to state dimensional properties (e.g., BRIGHT-

---

[1]Functions, unlike attributes and relations, do not take truth values but rather map objects onto other objects or values. For brevity, we sometimes use the term *predicate* to refer to all three categories: relations, attributes, and functions.

NESS(planet)). Relations are multiplace predicates that represent links between two or more entities, attributes, functions, or relations (e.g., REPELS(lodestone-1, lodestone-2); using magnetism as the domain).

To represent beliefs about physical domains, we use the qualitative process (QP) theory as a representation language (Forbus, 1984, 1990; Forbus & Gentner, 1986; Forbus, Nielsen, & Faltings, 1991; see Forbus, 1984, for a full description of the QP language and its model building capabilities). QP theory allows the representation of qualitative proportionalities between quantities and relations. For example, the statement QPROP + (a, b) expresses a positive qualitative relation between the quantities a and b: That is, that a is a monotonic positive function of (at least) b. QPROP – (a, b) expresses a negative qualitative relation.

Relations can hold between expressions as well as entities. Such higher order relations allow the construction of large representational structures that can describe, for example, the relation between magnetism and lodestone attraction:

IMPLIES(AND(MAGNETIC(lodestone-1), COMPOSED-OF(filing-1, iron)),
　　ATTRACTS(lodestone-1, filing-1))

It is the presence of structurally interconnected representations that is the key to implementing structure mapping. Given two representations in working memory, SME operates in a local-to-global manner to find one or a few structurally consistent matches. In the first stage, SME proposes matches between all identical predicates at any level (attribute, relation, higher order relation, etc.) in the two representations. At this stage, there may be many mutually inconsistent matches. In the next stage, these local correspondences are coalesced into large mappings, called *kernels,* by enforcing structural consistency (one-to-one mapping and parallel connectivity). SME allows correspondences between nonidentical entities and dimensions (represented as functions), in accordance with the principle that lower order information need not match identically. However, relations must match identically, reflecting the principle that comparison is implicitly directed toward finding structural commonality. For example, ATTRACTS(Sun, planet) may map to AT-TRACTS(magnet, nail), but can never map to COMPOSED-OF(nail, iron).

In the next step, SME gathers these structurally consistent clusters into one or a few global interpretations. At this point, it projects candidate inferences into the target. It does this by adding to the target representation any predicates that currently belong to the common structure in the base but are not yet present in the target. These predicates function as possible new inferences imported from the base to the target. The mappings are given a structural evaluation, reflecting the size and depth of the system of matches.

SME has many useful properties for modeling conceptual change. First, the final interpretation preserves large-scale connected structure. Second, this global interpretation does not need to be explicit at the outset. The assertions that will constitute the final point of the analogy need not be present initially in the target and need not have been extracted as a separable "goal structure" or "problem-solution structure" in the base before the comparison processes begins. SME begins blindly, using only local matches, and the final global interpretation emerges via the pull toward connectivity and systematicity in the later stages of the process. Third, SME makes spontaneous, structurally consistent inferences from its comparison process, unlike many other models of analogy (cf. Holyoak & Thagard, 1989; Markman, 1996). Finally, this model of the analogy process allows us to delineate four specific subprocesses that can change conceptual structure: highlighting, projection, re-representation, and restructuring (Gentner & Wolff, in press).

The Four Analogical Processes of Conceptual Change

Highlighting.   SME's first result is a matching system of predicates between the base and target. This models the psychological assumption that the process of alignment causes the matching aspects of the domains to become more salient (Elio & Anderson, 1981, 1984; Gentner & Wolff, in press; Gick & Holyoak, 1980, 1983; Markman & Gentner, 1993a, 1993b; Medin et al., 1993; Miller, 1979; Ortony, 1979). This process of highlighting is important because human representations, we suggest, are typically large, rich, and thickly interwoven nets of concepts. In particular, early representations tend to be conservative, in the sense that they retain many specific details of the context of learning: They are particularistic and contextually embedded (e.g., Brown, Collins, & Duguid, 1989; Forbus & Gentner, 1986; Medin & Ross, 1989). Highlighting can create a focus on a manageable subset of relevant information. Moreover, the relational identity constraint, combined with rerepresentation processes, means that the output of an analogy may reveal hitherto unnoticed relational commonalities. There is considerable psychological evidence that comparison can reveal nonobvious features (Gentner & Clement, 1988; Gentner & Imai, 1995; Markman & Gentner, 1993a; Medin et al., 1993; Ortony, Vondruska, Foss, & Jones, 1985; Tourangeau & Rips, 1991) and that highlighting of common information can influence category formation (Elio & Anderson, 1981, 1984; Medin & Ross, 1989; Ross, 1984, 1989; Skorstad, Gentner, & Medin, 1988).

Projection of candidate inferences.   As previously described, SME projects candidate inferences from the base to the target domain. These projected inferences, if accepted, add to the knowledge in the target domain. However, not all inferences made by SME will be correct. Postmapping processes, such as the application of semantic and pragmatic constraints, are necessary to ensure the correctness of the inferences (Falkenhainer, 1990; Kass, 1994; Kolodner, 1992, 1993; Novick & Holyoak, 1991).

Rerepresentation.   In rerepresentation, the representation of either or both domains is changed to improve the match. Typically, this involves a kind of tinkering in order that two initially mismatching predicates can be adjusted to match. For example, suppose an analogy matches well but for a mismatch between BRIGHTER-THAN(x,y) and FASTER-THAN(a,b) (as in Kepler's analogy that is discussed later). These relations can be rerepresented as GREATER-THAN(BRIGHT-NESS(x), BRIGHTNESS(y)), and GREATER-THAN(SPEED(a), SPEED(b)) to allow comparison. This involves a kind of decomposition that separates the GREATER-THAN magnitude relation (which is common to both) from the specific dimension of increase (which is distinctive). Studies of the development of children's comparison abilities support the psychological validity of such rerepresentation in learning: Children are better able to match cross-dimensional analogies when they have been induced to rerepresent the two situations to permit noticing the common magnitude increase (Gentner & Rattermann, 1991; Gentner, Rattermann, Markman, & Kotovsky, 1995; Kotovsky & Gentner, in press). We discuss SME's implementation of rerepresentation later in this article.

Restructuring.   Restructuring is the process of large-scale rearrangement of elements of the target domain to form a new coherent explanation. This rearrangement can take the form of adding or deleting causal links in the target domain as well as altering specific concepts. It should perhaps be considered separately from the other three processes or possibly as arising from a combination of the other three. For example, when little is known about a target domain, a mapping from the base can provide casual linkages that significantly alter the connectivity in the target. However, on this account, there must be some minimal alignment as a basis for inference; even if no initial relational match exists, there must be at least a partial object mapping (which could be suggested by local similarities or pragmatically stipulated; Forbus & Oblinger, 1990; Holyoak & Thagard, 1989; Winston, 1980). We conjecture that substantial restructuring during a single mapping is comparatively rare because normally the candidate inferences projected from the base domain will be at least compatible with the existing target structure. Furthermore, as Nersessian (1992) pointed out, massive restructuring from a single base can be dangerous: She noted that Faraday's modeling of magnetic fields by analogy with the concrete lines of iron filings created by magnets led to an overly concrete, partly erroneous model of the fields. In general, we suspect that most restructuring occurs as a result of multiple analogies iteratively applied as well as other processes. With these tools in hand, we now return to Kepler. We begin with some historical background.

KEPLER AND THE SOLAR SYSTEM

Kepler[2] (1571–1630) is best known today for his three laws of planetary motion.[3] His far more important contributions in changing our conception of the solar system are difficult to appreciate. Ironically, this is in part because of his very success. The conceptual structure that existed prior to Kepler's work is now almost impossible for us to call forth. Medieval cosmology differed from our own not only in the specific conceptual structure but also in the character of its explanations: They sought to find mathematical regularities, not causal mechanisms. It is here that Kepler's contribution lies. As Caspar (1993) put it: "It is Kepler's greatest service that he substituted a dynamic system for the formal schemes of the earlier astronomers, the law of nature for mathematical rule, and causal explanation for the mathematical description of motion" (p. 136). Holton (1973) went further: "Kepler's genius lies in his early search for a physics of the solar system. He is the first to look for a universal physical law based on terrestrial mechanics to comprehend the whole universe in its quantitative details" (p. 71).

To understand the magnitude of the conceptual change involved, an account of the prior state of belief is necessary.[4] Western cosmology in the 16th century, continuing the tradition laid down by the Greeks, stated the laws of planetary motion in purely mathematical terms. It postulated a universe with the Earth at the center,

---

[2]Opinions on Kepler's standing have varied. School children are taught that he was a mathematician who made his discoveries by trying all possible mathematical combinations, much in the manner of Langley, Bradshaw, and Simon's (1983) Bacon program. Koestler (1963) portrayed him as a neo-Platonic mystic, a "sleepwalker" who stumbled on his discoveries by accident. Many of his commentators consider that he ranks among the great scientists (e.g., Caspar, 1993; Gingerich, 1993; Holton, 1973; Koyre, 1973; Toulmin & Goodfield, 1961). Furthermore, as we make clear, he proceeded not by mechanical application of formulae but by the bold application of analogies and causal principles. This discussion of Kepler's work was compiled from a variety of sources: Barker (1991, 1993), Barker and Goldstein (1994), Baumgardt (1952), Butterfield (1957), Caspar (1993), Gingerich (1993), Hanson (1958), Holton (1973), Koestler (1963), Koyre (1973), Kuhn (1957), Layzer (1984), Mason (1962), Stephenson (1994a, 1994b), Toulmin and Goodfield (1961), and Vickers (1984)

[3]The first law states that the orbits of the planets are elliptical with the Sun at one focus. The second law (chronologically the first) states that the equal areas are swept in equal times by a line connecting a planet and the Sun. The third law states that the product of the square of the period of a planet's revolution and the cube of its mean distance from the Sun is constant.

[4]This account is taken chiefly from Butterfield (1957), Hanson (1958), Koyre (1973), Kuhn (1957), Layzer (1984), Mason (1962), Sambursky (1975), and Toulmin and Goodfield (1961). It is necessarily much abbreviated and oversimplified. There were dissenters, both among the Greeks—notably Aristarchus of Samos (310–230 B.C.), called "the Copernicus of Antiquity" for his heliocentric theory (Kuhn, 1957)—and in the Western scholastic tradition—including William of Ockham (1295–1349), who argued that postulating a spinning earth would simplify the explanations (an instance of Ockham's razor), Buridan (c. 1297–1358), Albert of Saxony (c. 1360), Oresme (c. 1323?–1382), and Nicolas of Cusa (1401–1464). However, even scholars willing to postulate a rotating earth did not generally countenance an earth that revolved around the Sun.

around which revolved crystalline spheres containing the heavenly bodies. The set of beliefs laid down by Plato and Aristotle and culminating in Ptolemy's system of the 2nd century A.D. was roughly as follows:

1. The Earth is at the center of the universe and is itself unmoving.

2. The Earth is surrounded by physically real crystalline spheres,[5] containing the heavenly bodies, which revolve around the Earth.

3. The heavenly bodies move in perfect circles at uniform velocity, as befits incorruptible bodies. (Epicycles and eccentrically positioned circles were admitted into the system to account for the observed motions.)

4. All motion requires a mover. The outermost sphere, containing the fixed stars, is moved by an "unmoved mover," the Primum Mobile. Each sphere imparts motion to the next one in; in the Aristotelian universe, there is no action-at-a-distance. In addition, each sphere is controlled by its own spirit that mediates its motion.[6] (The heavenly bodies were known not to move in synchrony.)

5. Celestial phenomena must be explained in entirely different terms from earthly phenomena. Indeed, heavenly bodies and their spheres are made of different matter altogether. They are composed not of the four terrestrial elements—earth, air, fire, and water—but instead of a fifth element (the quintessence), crystalline aether (pure, unalterable, transparent, and weightless). The further from Earth, the purer the sphere.

This Aristotelian–Ptolemaic system was integrated with Catholic theology, largely by Magnus (1206–1280) and Aquinas (1225–1274). Angelic spirits were assigned to the celestial spheres in order of rank: The outermost sphere, that of the Primum Mobile, belonged to the Seraphim; next inward, the Cherubim controlled the sphere of the fixed stars; next came Thrones, Dominations, Virtues, Powers, Principalities, Archangels, and finally Angels, who controlled the sphere of the moon. The resulting conceptual scheme, dominant until the 16th century, was one of extreme clarity, intricacy, and cohesion.

Thirteen centuries after Ptolemy's model, Copernicus (1473–1543) published (in 1543, the year of his death) *De Revolutionibus Orbium Celestium*, proposing the revolutionary idea that the Earth and other planets moved rather than the Sun.[7]

---

[5]There were variations on this basic scheme with different numbers of spheres. Aristotle's (384–322) system contained 55 spheres. However, when the Greek system was merged with Christian theology, the resulting system had 9 (or 10, depending on what is counted) spiritually significant spheres.

[6]In Aristotle's theory of motion, a homogeneous body required an external mover. There was a kind of analogy of the form *spirit | planet || soul | body || mover | moved.*

[7]Copernicus's theory was only partly heliocentric. For mathematical reasons, he placed the center of the solar system at the center of the Earth's orbit, rather than at the Sun itself.

Copernicus argued for his system on the grounds of mathematical elegance and sufficiency. He complained of the number of eccentric circles and epicycles required. He argued further that the Ptolemaic system had in effect departed from the ancient principle of perfect circularity and regularity of movement (by using "equants"—hypothetical points around which the centers of the planetary epicycles revolved—as a way of saving the fit to data).[8] The Copernican system was not widely accepted. Even among those learned enough to appreciate the problems with the Ptolemaic system, a more popular proposal was Brahe's system in which the five planets revolved around the Sun but the Sun itself revolved around a stationary Earth.

Kepler was a confirmed Copernican from the beginning, having studied the theory at Tubingen with Maestlin. In 1591, at the age of 20, he began as lecturer in mathematics at Graz. In his first book, the *Mysterium Cosmographicum,* in 1596, he defended the Copernican view and presented his own heliocentric proposal. The *Mysterium Cosmographicum* attracted the interest of Brahe (1546–1601), and in 1600 Kepler spent time as an assistant in Tycho's observatory. When Tycho died in 1601, Kepler was appointed his successor as Imperial Mathematician of the court in Prague.

Kepler acquired from Tycho the largest and most accurate store of astronomical observations available. He also acquired the task of determining the orbit of Mars, a task that proved far more difficult and ultimately more revealing than Kepler had foreseen. Kepler spent the next years trying to construct a consistent heliocentric model of the solar system based on his principle (discovered in the *Mysterium Cosmographicum*) that the planets move faster when closer to the Sun (a precursor of his second law, "equal area in equal times"). Unfortunately, he also retained the virtually universal, self-evident ancient principle that the orbits of the planets were perfect circles or were at least composed of perfect (although possibly eccentric) circles. Ultimately, the fact that his calculations for Mars's orbit differed from Tycho's observations (by the famous mere 8° of arc) forced him to a dismaying rejection of the ancient assumption of circularity. It is hard today to grasp how tenaciously these beliefs were held. Kepler, in the preface to the *Astronomia Nova,* commented on the incredible labor required to establish the existence of the solar force, largely due to the power of the assumption of circular motion "because I had bound them to the millstones (as it were) of circularity, under the spell of common opinion. Restrained by such fetters, the movers could not do their work" (p. 67).[9]

---

[8]In fact, although Copernicus was able to divest himself of the "major epicycles" that accounted for the planets' apparent retrograde motions and of the notion of the *equant* (an imaginary point from which the calculated orbit would appear more uniform), he was forced to maintain a complex set of eccentrics and minor epicycles (34 circles in all) as compared with Kepler's six ellipses (Mason, 1962).

[9]Galileo (1564–1642), Kepler's brilliant contemporary and a fellow Copernican, never abandoned the belief that the planets moved in perfect circles at uniform velocity, despite receiving Kepler's evidence for elliptical orbits.

He next tried fruitlessly to model the planetary path with an ovoid, before at last accepting the ellipse as the shape of the orbit.[10] This led to a more precise statement of the Second Law of planetary motion, that a line between the Sun and any planet sweeps out equal areas in equal intervals of time and to the First Law, that the planetary orbits are ellipses with the Sun at one focus.[11] With this new model Kepler could replace Copernicus's 34 circles with just six ellipses.[12]

Kepler published this new view in 1609 as the *Astronomia Nova: A New Astronomy Based on Causation, or a Physics of the Sky*. It records the discoveries and the saga of his quest to derive the orbit of the planets—in particular, Mars, the most resistant to calculation—from causal principles.[13] He understood well that his causal explanation moved him out of the kind of astronomy practiced at the time and announced in the introductory summary: "Ye physicists, prick your ears, for now we are going to invade your territory" (as cited in Koestler, 1963, p. 325). Kepler's causal explanation of planetary motion and his three laws were a major step toward our modern conception of the solar system. As Gingerich (1993) put it:

Kepler's most consequential achievement was the mechanizing and perfecting of the world system. By the *mechanization* of the solar system, I mean his insistence on "a new astronomy based on causes, or the celestial physics," as he tells us in the title of his great book. By the *perfection* of the planetary system, I mean the fantastic improvement of nearly two orders of magnitude in the prediction of planetary positions. (p. 333)[14]

We now return to the beginning, to the *Mysterium Cosmographicum* (1596), to ask how Kepler arrived at this revolutionary position. One last bit of context setting is necessary. Besides Copernicus's treatise, there were two astronomical events, both solidly documented by Brahe, that helped to prepare the ground for new conceptions of the heavens. The first was a nova (or supernova) in 1572. The

---

[10]After abandoning the circle, Kepler at first used the ellipse merely as a mathematical approximation to the ovoid, or egg, which had the advantage of possessing only one focus. He resisted the ellipse as a solution for physical reasons: If the Sun was the unique cause of planetary motion, then there should be one unique place for it, not an arbitrary selection from between two foci as with an ellipse (Hanson, 1958).

[11]The Second Law appears in rough form in the *Mysterium Cosmographicum* (1596) and appears explicitly in Book III of the *Astronomia Nova*, before the First Law in Book IV. It was in fact crucial to his derivation of the First and Third Laws. The Third Law appears in the *Harmonice Mundi* in 1619.

[12]However, Kepler's system was not accepted by his contemporaries. Even those few willing to consider Kepler's and Copernicus's heliocentric views (including Kepler's old mentor, Maestlin) rejected his notion of a celestial physics governed by the same causal law as earthly phenomena.

[13]Hanson (1958), echoing Charles Sanders Peirce, called Kepler's discovery of the orbit of Mars "the greatest piece of retroductive reasoning ever performed" (p. 85).

[14]Gingerich (1993) noted that it was the success of these predictions (the Rudophine Tables) that kept Kepler's theory alive during the 2 centuries after its publication.

addition of a new fixed star was evidence against the Aristotelian doctrine of the unchanging and incorruptible firmament. The second was a comet in 1577 (and others not long after), whose path ran through the planetary spheres and which challenged the physical reality of the crystalline spheres. Fueled in part by these challenges to Aristotelian cosmology, there was a revival of the Stoic cosmology in the late 16th century (see Barker, 1991, for a more detailed account). Like the Aristotelian view, the Stoic view was geocentric and had a sphere of fixed stars; it differed in that it postulated that the heavens were filled not with pure aether but with a kind of intelligent pneuma (a combination of fire and air), which became more pure with distance from the earth. The heavenly bodies, made of pneuma, were intelligent and capable of self-direction. Although Kepler firmly dismissed the view that the planets were each attached to their own crystalline spheres, he continued to wrestle with the idea that the planets move themselves intelligently.

The Sun as Prime Mover: The Light–*Anima Motrix* Analogy

As Toulmin and Goodfield (1961) put it:

> The lifelong, self-appointed mission of Johann Kepler ... was to reveal the new, inner coherence of the Sun-centered planetary system. His central aim was to produce a "celestial physics," a system of astronomy of a new kind, in which the forces responsible for the phenomena were brought to light. (p. 198)

Kepler combined a neo-Platonist's love of mathematical regularity, a commitment to explanation in terms of physical causation, and an equally strong belief in empirical tests. In the preface to the *Mysterium Cosmographicum*, the 25-year-old Kepler stated his purpose: "There were three things of which I persistently sought the reasons why they were such and not otherwise: the number, size and motion of the circles" (Kepler, 1596/1981, p. 63).

Kepler's solution to the first two questions was a system of inscribed solids that predicted the distances of the planets from the Sun (see Figure 1). This is a rather quixotic model that clearly shows Kepler's passion for mathematically regularities. The extreme particularity of this initial model is striking: The distance of a given planet from the Sun could only be calculated by knowing the orbit of the next inward planet.

The work is interesting in at least two more respects. The first is Kepler's reworking of the Copernican theory to be more consistently heliocentric. Rejecting the Copernican placement of the center of the solar system as at the center of the Earth's orbit, Kepler proposed a mathematically small but physically significant change: The center of the solar system was the Sun itself. As Aiton (1976) pointed out, Kepler's causal interpretation of Copernicus's theory led to a reaxiomitization

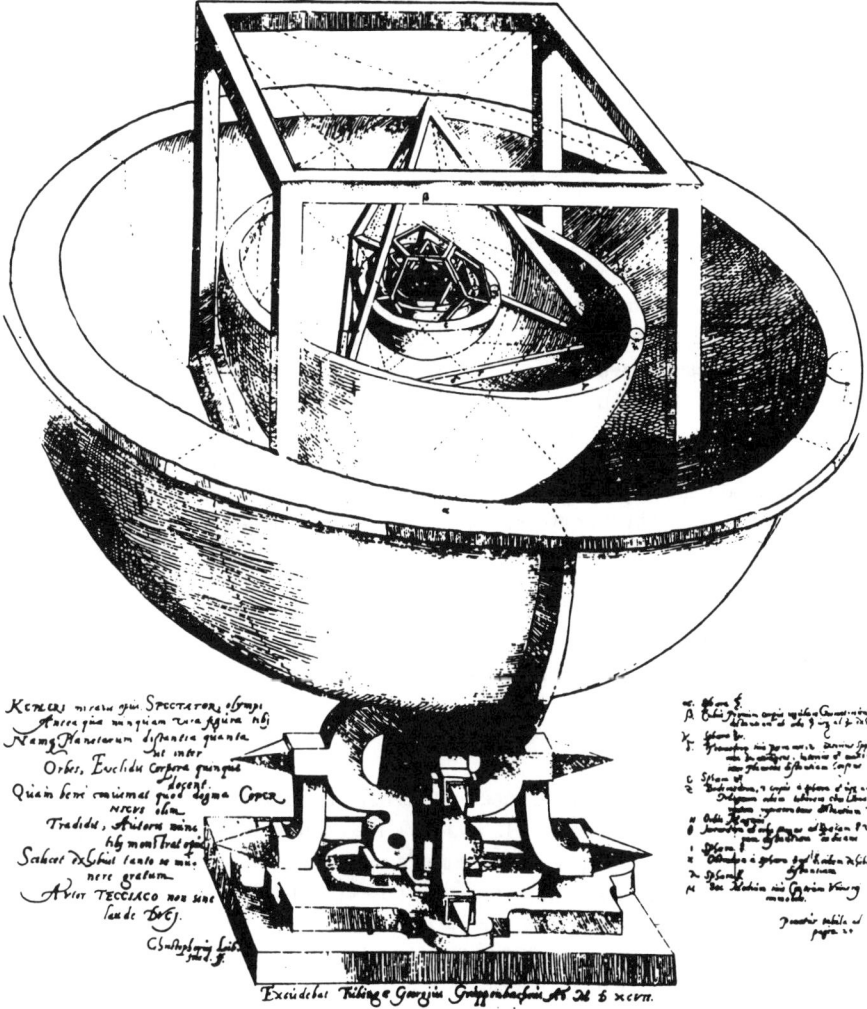

Johannes Kepler, *Mysterium cosmographicum*. Copper engraving
from the first edition (Tübingen, 1596).

FIGURE 1 Kepler's model of the solar system from the *Mysterium Cosmographicum*,
showing the inscribed solids. From *Mysterium Cosmographicum I, II* (p. 1), by J. Kepler, 1981,
New York: Abaris Books. Copyright by Abaris Books, Norwalk, CT. Reprinted with permission.

of astronomy. Kepler also posed an important question. He noticed that the periods of the outer planets were longer, relative to those of the inner planets, than could be predicted simply from the greater distances they had to travel. That is, the planets further away from the Sun moved slower than those closer to the Sun. Were the moving souls simply weaker in the faraway planets? Kepler reasoned:

> One of two conclusions must be reached: either the moving souls [*motricis animae*] are weaker the further they are from the Sun; or, there is a single moving soul [*motricem animam*][15] in the center of all the spheres, that is, in the Sun, and it impels each body more strongly in proportion to how near it is. (Kepler, 1596/1981, p. 199)

Kepler went on to apply this hypothesis to the paths of the individual planets. If motion is caused by a single *anima motrix* in the Sun that weakens with distance, this would explain why each individual planet should move slower when further from the Sun. (This insight requires noting the nonuniform speed of the planets, a fact that emerges only when the observations are recast from Ptolemaian epicycles into a heliocentric system.) To reason further, he used an analogy with light:

> Let us suppose, then, as is highly probable, that motion is dispensed by the Sun in the same proportion as light. Now the ratio in which light spreading out from a center is weakened is stated by the opticians. For the amount of light in a small circle is the same as the amount of light or of the solar rays in the great one. Hence, as it is more concentrated in the small circle, and more thinly spread in the great one, the measure of this thinning out must be sought in the actual ratio of the circles, both for light and for the moving power [*motrice virtute*]. (Kepler, 1596/1981, p. 201)

Pushing the Analogy

Kepler returned repeatedly to the analogy between light and the motive power. In the *Mysterium cosmographicum* (1596/1981), the analogy functioned as a kind of existence proof that the Sun's influence could be assumed to weaken in an orderly way with distance. Kepler's many subsequent uses of this analogy served to extend and refine this notion of the *vis motrix*. He devoted multiple chapters of his greatest work, the *Astronomia Nova* (1609/1992) to its explanation and returned to it again in the *Epitome of Copernican Astronomy* (1621/1969). Kepler also delved into the domain of light and optics. He published a treatise on astronomical optics *Astronomiae Pars Optica* in 1604 and another piece on optics, the *Dioptrice* in 1611.

---

[15]Kepler's annotation in 1621/1981 stated: "If for the word 'soul' [*Anima*] you substitute the word 'force' [*Vim*], you have the very same principle on which the Celestial Physics is established" (p. 201). (We return to this shift from *soul* to *force* in the Discussion section.)

With this knowledge of the behavior of light, Kepler had a base domain systematic enough to provide considerable inferential resources for the target (Bassok & Holyoak, 1989; Bowdle & Gentner, 1996; Clement & Gentner, 1991; Gentner & Bowdle, 1994; Gentner & Gentner, 1983).

In the *Astronomia Nova,* Kepler developed this analogy of motive power with light much further. Early on, he raised the challenge of action at a distance:

> For it was said above that this motive power is extended throughout the space of the world, in some places more concentrated and in others more spread out. ... This implies that it is poured out throughout the whole world, and yet does not exist anywhere but where there is something movable. (Kepler, 1609/1992, p. 382)

He answered this challenge by invoking the light analogy.

> But lest I appear to philosophize with excessive insolence, I shall propose to the reader the clearly authentic example of light, since it also makes its nest in the Sun, thence to break forth into the whole world as a companion to this motive power. Who, I ask, will say that light is something material? Nevertheless, it carries out its operations with respect to place, suffers alteration, is reflected and refracted, and assumes quantities so as to be dense or rare, and to be capable of being taken as a surface wherever it falls upon something illuminable. Now just as it is said in optics, that light does not exist in the intermediate space between the source and the illuminable, this is equally true of the motive power. (Kepler, 1609/1992, p. 383)

Kepler also used the light analogy to buttress a prior claim, namely, that the *vis motrix* is diminished with distance not through being lost but through being spread out (a kind of conservation principle). He used two further potential analogs here: odors and heat. These are near misses (Winston, 1980), which differ with respect to the key behavior and thus serve to sharpen the parallel between light and the *vis motrix.*

> Since there is just as much power in a larger and more distant circle as there is in a smaller and closer one, nothing of this power is lost in traveling from its source, nothing is scattered between the source and the movable body. The emission, then, in the same manner as light, is immaterial, unlike odours, which are accompanied by a diminution of substance, and unlike heat from a hot furnace, or anything similar which fills the intervening space. (Kepler, 1609/1992, p. 381)

To trace the analogical process, we represented parts of Kepler's expressed knowledge about light and the motive power. We applied SME to these representations to simulate the process of analogical reasoning that Kepler may have used in rethinking his conceptual model of the solar system.

Our representation of Kepler's knowledge of the nature of light[16] is shown in Figure 2. Specifically, we ascribe to Kepler five beliefs: (a) A source produces light that travels instantaneously and undetectibly through space until it reaches an object, at which point the light is detectable; (b) the brightness of an object decreases with distance from a source; (c) the concentration of light affects the brightness of an object, with a greater concentration resulting in greater brightness; (d) as light spreads from a source there is an increase in volume and a decrease in concentration so that multiplying the volume by the concentration will produce a constant; and hence, (e) the concentration of light decreases as an object's distance from the source increases.

Kepler's initial knowledge of the motive power was of course considerably less rich than his knowledge about light. In our representation of this knowledge (see Figure 3), we use the term *vis motrix,* reflecting Kepler's shift to calling the Sun's influence *virtus motrix* or *vis motrix* (motive power or motive force) rather than *anima motrix* (motive spirit). His terminology over time had become less animate and more mechanical.

The *Vis Motrix* Analogy and the Process of Conceptual Change

Highlighting.   When given these representations of Kepler's knowledge of light and of the Sun's motive force, SME produces the interpretation shown in Figure 4. This interpretation highlights commonalities, for example, the similarity that in both cases the emanation makes itself known when it strikes a planet and, respectively, illuminates or moves the planet.

Projection.   As we have noted, highlighting influences conceptual change in part by identifying relevant aspects of the two domains and thereby permitting abstraction. It also provides the alignable structure over which two other processes of conceptual change operate: projection and rerepresentation. This is crucial, for by constraining the candidate inferences to be those connected to the aligned structure we can model an inferential process that is generative without overshooting into "wanton inferencing" (Eric Diettrich, personal communication, February 1994). The *vis motrix*–light analogy leads to several candidate inferences. Figure 5 shows SME's inferences, which seem reasonably like those Kepler appears to have made. First, SME infers that the *vis motrix* travels from the Sun to the planet through space. Second, it infers that the product of volume and concentration of

---

[16]These representations are of course not intended to be exhaustive representations of Kepler's knowledge but of the subset necessary to make our points about analogy and conceptual change. We do not attempt a full explanation of how Kepler selected the relevant information from his larger knowledge of light. Although this is clearly important, it is beyond the scope of this article.

2a:

(PRODUCE Sun light)

(CAUSE (TRAVEL light Sun object space)
      (REACH light object))

(INSTANTANEOUS (TRAVEL light Sun object space))

(WHILE (AND (TRAVEL light Sun object space)
          (NOT (REACH light object)))
      (NOT (DETECTABLE light)))

(WHILE (AND (TRAVEL light Sun object space)
          (REACH light object))
      (DETECTABLE light))

2b:

(QPROP- (CONCENTRATION light object)
      (DISTANCE object Sun))

2c:

(CAUSE (REACH light object)
      (PROMOTE (BRIGHTNESS object)))

(QPROP+ (BRIGHTNESS object)
      (CONCENTRATION light object))

2d:

(CAUSE (AND (QPROP+ (VOLUME light)
           (DISTANCE Sun object))
        (QPROP- (CONCENTRATION light object)
           (DISTANCE object Sun)))
      (CONSTANT (* (VOLUME light)
          (CONCENTRATION light object))))

(continued)

2e:

$$\text{(IMPLIES (AND (QPROP- (CONCENTRATION light object)}$$
$$\text{(DISTANCE object Sun))}$$
$$\text{(QPROP+ (BRIGHTNESS object)}$$
$$\text{(CONCENTRATION light object)))}$$
$$\text{(QPROP- (BRIGHTNESS object)}$$
$$\text{(DISTANCE object Sun)))}$$

FIGURE 2   Schematic representation of the belief structure for light in the light–*vis motrix* analogy.

3a:

$$\text{(CAUSE (REACH vis-motrix planet)}$$
$$\text{(PROMOTE (SPEED planet)))}$$

3b:

FIGURE 3   Schematic representation of the *vis motrix* beliefs.

$$\text{(QPROP- (SPEED planet)}$$
$$\text{(DISTANCE planet Sun))}$$

4:

$$\text{(CAUSE (REACH light object)}$$
$$\text{(PROMOTE (BRIGHTNESS object)))}$$

$$\text{(CAUSE (REACH vis-motrix planet)}$$
$$\text{(PROMOTE (SPEED planet)))}$$

$$\text{(QPROP- (BRIGHTNESS object)}$$
$$\text{(DISTANCE object Sun))}$$

$$\text{(QPROP- (SPEED planet)}$$
$$\text{(DISTANCE planet Sun))}$$

FIGURE 4   Structure-mapping engine interpretation for the light–*vis motrix* analogy.

the *vis motrix* is a constant. Third, SME explains that because the concentration of the *vis motrix* decreases with distance, and the concentration of the *vis motrix* governs the speed of the planet, the speed of the planet will decrease with distance from the Sun. Finally, SME infers that the *vis motrix* will be detectable once it contacts the planet but not while it travels to the planet (the last two inferences shown in Figure 5). Taken together, these inferences explain the apparent phenomenon of action at a distance.

Rerepresentation.   We suggested that the process of alignment can lead to rerepresentating parts of one or both representations in such a way as to improve the alignment. Figure 6 shows this process as well as highlighting and projecting inferences. Such a process may have operated on a large scale to contribute to Kepler's gradual shift toward thinking of the motive power as a physical phenomenon rather than an animistic one. However, a more locally contained example can be found shortly after the passage quoted previously in the *Astronomia Nova*. Kepler noted a discrepancy—an important alignable difference—and tried to resolve it:

> Moreover, although light itself does indeed flow forth in no time, while this power creates motion in time, nonetheless the way in which both do so is the same, if you consider them correctly. Light manifests those things which are proper to it instantaneously, but requires time to effect those which are associated with matter. It illuminates a surface in a moment, because here matter need not undergo any alteration, for all illumination takes place according to surfaces, or at least as if a property of surfaces and not as a property of corporeality as such. On the other hand, light bleaches colours in time, since here it acts upon matter qua matter, making it hot and expelling the contrary cold which is embedded in the body's matter and is not on

5:
(CAUSE (TRAVEL vis-motrix Sun planet (:SKOLEM space))
     (REACH vis-motrix planet))

(CAUSE (AND (QPROP+ (VOLUME (:SKOLEM space))
           (DISTANCE Sun planet))
     (QPROP- (CONCENTRATION vis-motrix planet)
          (DISTANCE planet Sun)))
    (CONSTANT (* (VOLUME (:SKOLEM space))
        (CONCENTRATION vis-motrix planet)))))

(IMPLIES (AND (QPROP- (CONCENTRATION vis-motrix planet)
         (DISTANCE planet Sun))
    (QPROP+ (SPEED planet)
        (CONCENTRATION vis-motrix planet)))
  (QPROP- (SPEED planet) (DISTANCE planet Sun)))

(WHILE (AND (TRAVEL vis-motrix Sun planet (:SKOLEM space))
    (NOT (REACH vis-motrix planet)))
  (NOT (DETECTABLE vis-motrix)))

(WHILE (AND (TRAVEL vis-motrix Sun planet (:SKOLEM space))
    (REACH vis-motrix planet))
  (DETECTABLE vis-motrix))

FIGURE 5   Structure-mapping engine's candidate inferences for the light–*vis motrix* analogy.

Analogical mapping can change representation(s)

Selecting/Highlighting (Matching/Alignment)

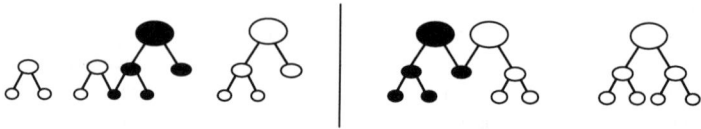

*Candidate Inferences (Transfer)

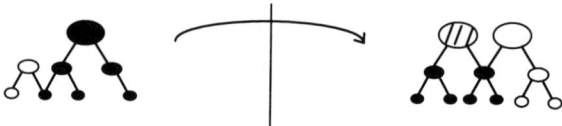

*Re-representation (Provisional alteration to improve match)

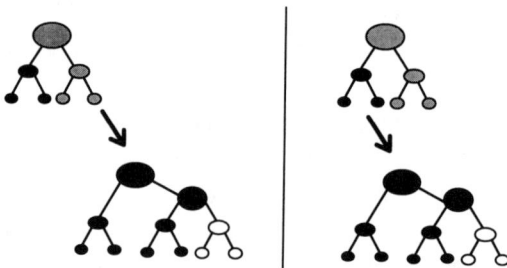

FIGURE 6   Ways analogy can create change.

its surface. In precisely the same manner, this moving power perpetually and without any interval of time is present from the Sun wherever there is a suitable movable body, for it receives nothing from the movable body to cause it to be there. On the other hand, it causes motion in time, since the movable body is material. (Kepler, 1609/1992, p. 383)

Kepler believed (according to the conventional wisdom of the time) that light moved instantaneously from the Sun to light up the planets:

INSTANTANEOUS (AFFECT (light, Sun, planet, space))

However, he believed that the *vis motrix* required time to affect the motion of the planets. At a rough level, then, Kepler faced a mismatch between the candidate inference from light and his existing knowledge about the planetary motion:

INSTANTANEOUS (AFFECT (*vis-motrix,* Sun, planet, space))
TIME-OCCURRING (AFFECT (*vis-motrix,* Sun, planet, space))

Kepler (1609/1992) admitted the problem but suggested a rerepresentation "although light itself does indeed flow forth in no time, while this power creates motion in time, nonetheless the way in which both do so is the same, if you consider them correctly" (p. 383). His solution was to be more precise about the notion of AFFECT (influence, planet). For such an effect to occur, he reasoned, the influence must travel to the planet and interact with the planet somehow. Kepler suggested that travel is instantaneous for both kinds of influences (the *vis motrix* and light). However, whereas light need only interact with the surfaces of bodies to illuminate them (which, Kepler believed, can be done instantaneously), the *vis motrix* must interact with the body of the planet itself to cause motion, and this requires time. Thus, Kepler gained a partial identity by decomposing and rerepresenting the previously nonmatching statements. Instead of the nonmatching pair:

INSTANTANEOUS (AFFECT (*vis-motrix,* Sun, planet, space)
TIME-OCCURING (AFFECT (*vis-motrix,* Sun, planet, space)

he now had the partial match:

INSTANTANEOUS (TRAVEL (light, Sun, planet, space))
INSTANTANEOUS (PROMOTE (BRIGHTNESS (planet)))

INSTANTANEOUS (TRAVEL (*vis-motrix,* Sun, planet, space))
TIME-OCCURRING (PROMOTE (SPEED (planet)))

Alignable differences.   Given a structural alignment, connected differences become salient. Kepler used these differences to deal with the question of whether the Sun's light and the motive power may in fact be the same thing (a reasonable question given the force of the analogy). He answered that they cannot be the same, because light can be impeded by an opaque blocker (e.g., during an eclipse), yet the motive power is not thereby impeded (otherwise motion would stop during an eclipse; see Figure 7):

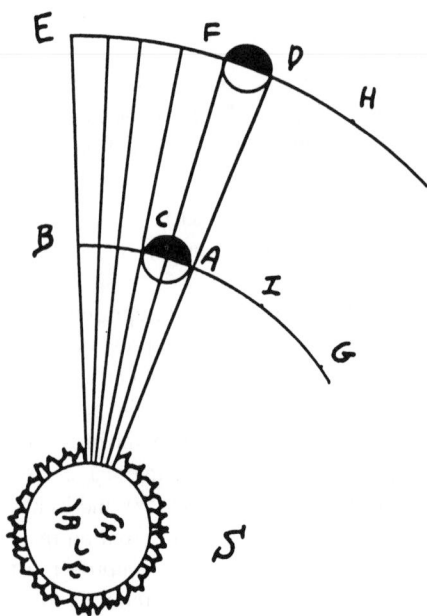

FIGURE 7   Kepler's depiction of the Sun's light radiating outward. From *Epitome of Copernican Astronomy* (p. 103), by J. Kepler, 1618/1969, New York: Kraus Reprint. Copyright by St. John's College Press, Annapolis, MD. Reprinted with permission.

The analogy between light and motive power is not to be disturbed by rashly confusing their properties. Light is impeded by the opaque, but is not impeded by a body. ... Power acts upon the body without respect to its opacity. Therefore, since it is not correlated with the opaque, it is likewise not impeded by the opaque. (Kepler, 1609/1992, p. 392)

A more important alignable difference concerns the degree of decrease with distance. By the time of the *Astronomia Nova,* Kepler was clear about the fact that the concentration of light diminishes as the inverse square of distance from its source. He therefore held himself responsible for either mapping this fact into the target, or explaining why it should not be mapped. As it happens, he still required a simple inverse law for the *vis motrix,* because in his model the *vis motrix* directly caused the planetary motion.[17] As usual, he tackled this discrepancy head on and

---

[17]Kepler's dynamics was Aristotelian: He believed that velocity was caused by (and proportional to) the motive force (as opposed to the Newtonian view that forces cause *changes* in velocity). He held the belief of his time that the planets would cease to move if not pushed around that the Sun. Thus, he conceived of the motive force as acting directly to impart counterclockwise speed to the planets (rather than imparting inward acceleration, as in Newton's system). As Koestler (1963) noted, Kepler had made the insightful move of decomposing planetary motion into two separate components, but had reversed the roles of gravity and planetary inertia. Kepler thought that the planets' forward motion was caused by the Sun and their inward motion by magnetism specific to each planet. In the Newtonian system, the planets' inward motion is caused by the Sun, and their forward motion by inertia specific to each planet.

produced, in the *Astronomia Nova,* a long mathematical argument that, because the *vis motrix* can cause motion only in planes perpendicular to the Sun's axis of rotation, the proper analog to the *vis motrix* is light spreading out not in a sphere around the Sun, but only in a plane. Thus, he justified the alignable difference that the concentration of *vis motrix* should decrease as a simple inverse of distance, even though the concentration of light decreases with inverse-square distance.

Restructuring.   From what we have said so far, it appears that the *vis motrix* analogy may have contributed to Kepler's restructuring of his model of the solar system. It provided him with a structure from which to argue for a single causal "soul" in the Sun, rather than moving souls in each of the planets, and to the gradual mechanization of this soul to a power or force. The analogy may also have promoted the shift from crystalline spheres containing the planets to paths continually negotiated between the Sun and the planets. We return to this issue in the Discussion section.

RICHER ASPECTS OF THE ANALOGICAL PROCESS

The analogy between the *vis motrix* and light provides insight into some aspects of Kepler's conceptual change. However, this analogy is part of a much larger process. Kepler used several other analogies—including a sailor steering a ship, a balance scale, and a magnet. Some of these were used only once or twice, but at least one other was intensely developed and extended. This was an analogy between the *vis motrix* and magnetism, which Kepler used to reason out aspects of the phenomenon that the analogy with light could not explain. He modeled the planets and the Sun as magnets and tried to explain the inward and outward movements of the planets in terms of attractions and repulsions resulting from which poles were proximate.[18]

Although it is beyond the scope of this article to provide a full model of the development of Kepler's thought, at least three additional mechanisms are needed to capture his analogy process. First, a mechanism is needed to mediate between multiple analogies. For example, how did Kepler intersect the magnetism mapping (which explained why a planet varied in distance from the Sun in terms of alternating attraction and repulsion between two magnets that revolve around one another) with the light analogy? One computational approach may be found in Burstein's (1986) CARL, which combined different analogies to build a repre-

---

[18]By the time of the *Astronomia Nova* in 1609, Kepler had become familiar with the work of William Gilbert (*De Magnete,* 1600) and drew extensively on Gilbert's proposal that the Earth may function as a giant magnet. Kepler's analogy went further in applying this model to the Sun and planets. Interestingly, although Gilbert believed that the Earth rotated on its axis, he retained a Tychonic model in which the Sun and its satellite planets revolved around the Earth.

sentation of how a variable works. Spiro, Feltovich, Coulson, and Anderson (1989) have also traced the way in which multiple analogies are combined to produce a domain model.

A second mechanism needed is incremental analogizing. As new information about a domain is learned or brought in, the system must be able to extend the original mapping. It has been shown that participants are sensitive to a recent mapping, and will more quickly extend that mapping than create a new one (Boronat & Gentner, 1996; Gentner & Boronat, 1992). A few incremental analogical mapping models exist (Burstein, 1986; Keane, 1990), including an incremental version of SME (ISME), which can extend an analogy after the initial mapping has been made (Forbus, Ferguson, & Gentner, 1994). ISME draws further information from its long term knowledge to add to the working memory descriptions. It then remaps the analogy, building on the results of the initial mapping, thus enriching the overall analogical mapping. ISME can model the process of extended analogizing in problem solving, and we think it has promise for capturing creative extension processes.

Finally, it should be possible to embed these mapping processes in a process that can test the projected inferences of the mapping and make rerepresentations when needed. The system that comes closest to this is PHINEAS (Falkenhainer, 1990), which constructs physical theories by analogy with previously understood examples, by iterating through what Falkenhainer called a map–analyze cycle. In this cycle, PHINEAS starts with a qualitative description of a physical systems behavior and a set of domain theories. If it does not have an applicable theory to explain the new behavior, then it uses analogy to find an explanation. PHINEAS has an index of previously explained examples, arranged using an abstraction hierarchy of observed behaviors. PHINEAS selects and evaluates potentially analogous examples from this hierarchy and then uses SME to generate a set of correspondences between the novel behavior and the understood example. The explanation for the new behavior is then projected from the explanation of the old behavior. PHINEAS then tests this new explanation to make sure that it is coherent with its rules about physical domains. When there is conflict, Phineas can rerepresent some predicates. It then simulates the operation of the new theory to replicate the observed behavior.

DISCUSSION

Kepler used analogies both widely and deeply in his quest for an understanding of planetary motion. We have traced some of these analogies and modeled the processes using SME. We suggest that these analogies were instrumental to Kepler's conceptual change. To argue this point, we must justify some key assumptions.

Did Kepler Use Analogy in Thinking?

The frequent use of analogies in Kepler's texts is no guarantee that these analogies drove his conceptual change. He could have used analogy simply as a rhetorical device. Although there is no way to decide this issue definitively, there are reasons to believe that at least some of Kepler's analogies were instrumental in his thought processes. First, as discussed earlier, his major analogies were pursued with almost fanatical intensity across and within his major works. There are numerous detailed diagrams of base and target, long passages that spell out the commonalities, the inferences, and the incremental extensions, as well as alignable differences between base and target and Kepler's assessment of their import.

The open and inclusive character of Kepler's general writing practice offers a second line of encouragement for the belief that the extended analogies used in his text were actually used in his thought processes. Many of Kepler's commentators note the exceptional—at times even excessive—candor and detail of his scientific writing. Holton (1973), in noting that Kepler was relatively neglected among the great early scientists, stated:

> [Modern scientists are] taught to hide behind a rigorous structure the actual steps of discovery—those guesses, errors, and occasional strokes of good luck without which creative scientific work does not usually occur. But Kepler's embarrassing candor and intense emotional involvement force him to give us a detailed account of his tortuous process. ... He gives us lengthy accounts of his failures, though sometimes they are tinged with ill-concealed pride in the difficulty of his task. With rich imagination he frequently finds analogies from every phase of life, exalted or commonplace. He is apt to interrupt his scientific thoughts, either with exhortations to the reader to follow a little longer through the almost unreadable account, or with trivial side issues and textual quibbling, or with personal anecdotes or delighted exclamations about some new geometrical relation, a numerological or musical analogy. (pp. 69–70)

Kepler's writings are studded with personal comments that would be inadmissible in modern papers: "In what follows, the reader should overlook my credulity, since I am judging everything by my own wits." (Kepler, 1609/1992, p. 95); "Consider, thoughtful reader, and you will be transfixed by the force of the argument" (Kepler, 1609/1992, p. 290); and "And we, good reader, will not indulge in this splendid triumph for more than one small day ... restrained as we are by the rumours of a new rebellion, lest the fabric of our achievement perish with excessive rejoicing" (Kepler, 1609/1992, p. 290). On this last occasion, Kepler's foreboding proved correct, for he was then working on an egg-shaped orbit which proved a failure. When he at last rejected the egg in favor of the ellipse (hitherto used only as a mathematical approximation) he again reacted feelingly: "O me ridiculum!

[How ridiculous of me!]: As though the libration in diameter could not lead to the elliptical path" (as cited in Hanson, 1958, p. 83).

Kepler's (1609/1992) inclusiveness stemmed in part from his interest in "the roads by which men arrive at their insights into celestial matters" (as cited in Koestler, 1963, p. 261). In the introduction to the *Astronomia Nova,* he stated this agenda explicitly:

> Here it is a question not only of leading the reader to an understanding of the subject matter in the easiest way, but also, chiefly, of the arguments, meanderings, or even chance occurrences by which I the author first came upon that understanding. (Kepler, 1609/1992, p. 78)[19]

His writings include long sections detailing calculations made in pursuit of false assumptions; often the hapless reader is only informed afterwards that this effort has been misguided. A similar example occurred with the publication in 1621 of the second edition of his first book, the *Mysterium Cosmographicum* (1596/1981). Kepler's ideas had changed radically in the 25 intervening years, yet he chose not to rewrite but to leave the original text intact, adding notes that specified how and why his ideas had changed. The annotations in 1621 again reveal a zest for tracing the cognitive paths of discovery:

> The remaining hints at the truth that are offered by erroneous values, and which I quote everywhere, are fortuitous, but do not deserve to be deleted; yet I enjoy recognizing them, because they tell me by what meanders, and by feeling along what walls through the darkness of ignorance, I have reached the shining gateway of truth. (Kepler, 1621/1981, p. 215)

Even if some of Kepler's analogies are later additions, it seems likely that many of them formed a serious part of his journey.

A third indication that Kepler may have used analogies in thinking is that the sheer fecundity of his analogizing, suggests that analogy was a natural mode of thought for him. In the *Epitome of Copernican Astronomy* (1621/1969), he likened the Earth to a spinning top to answer why it revolves only in one direction. Later (Kepler, 1621/1969), he compared his celestial physics—in which planetary paths arise out of interacting forces—with the fixed firmament of the ancients:

> Here we entrust the planet to the river, with an oblique rudder, by the help of which the planet, while floating down, may cross from one bank to the opposite. But the ancient astronomy built a solid bridge—the solid spheres—above this river,—the

---

[19]However, Stephenson (1994a), although noting the "almost confessional style" of the *Astronomia Nova,* argued that Kepler shaped the book in this way to persuade astronomers of his new views.

latitude of the zodiac—and transports the lifeless planet along the bridge as if in a chariot. But if the whole contrivance is examined carefully, it appears that this bridge has no props by which it is supported, not does it rest upon the earth, which they believed to be the foundation of the heavens. (pp. 182–183)

In pursuit of a causal model of the planetary system, Kepler analogized Sun and planet to sailors in a river, magnets, and orators gazing at a crowd, among other domains. Analogies are used for matters personal as well as public, playful as well as serious. For example, he wrote Fabricius in 1608, criticizing his (Fabricius's) model: "You say that geometry bore you a daughter. I looked at her, she is beautiful, but she will become a very bad wench who will seduce all the men of the many daughters which mother physics has borne me." During one of his frequent bouts of financial travails (as Imperial Mathematician, he held a post of high honor and intermittent renumeration) he wrote a friend: "My hungry stomach looks up like a little dog to the master who once fed it" (as cited in Caspar, 1993, p. 157).

A fourth reason to take Kepler's analogies seriously is that he himself did so. This is apparent from his explicit comments. For example, Vickers (1984) discussed how in the *Optics* (1904), Kepler treated the conic sections by analogy with light through a lens. Kepler justified this unorthodox treatment as follows:

But for us the terms in Geometry should serve the analogy (for I especially love analogies, my most faithful masters, acquainted with all the secrets of nature) and one should make great use of them in geometry, where—despite the incongruous terminology—they bring the solution of an infinity of cases lying between the extreme and the man, and where they clearly present to our eyes the whole essence of the question. (pp 149–150)

Kepler does not, however, consider analogy a substitute for logical proof: "Analogy has shown, and Geometry confirms" (p. 150).

What Did Kepler Mean by "Analogy"?

Alchemy, the dominant approach to natural phenomena in medieval Europe, was still a major presence during Kepler's life. The alchemists used analogies and metaphors in great quantity and relied on them as a guide to truth. Yet, from the viewpoint of current scientific practice, their use of analogy was wildly unconstrained. Many-to-one mappings and other structural inconsistencies were normal practice. Richness and ambiguity, rather than clarity and systematicity, were valued (see Gentner & Jeziorski, 1993, for a comparison of alchemical analogies with current scientific analogies). A final indication of how seriously Kepler took analogy was his sharp criticisms of this sort of analogizing, which stand in striking contrast to his normal collegial charity. In the *Harmonice Mundi* (1619) he strove to distinguish the proper use of analogy from the methods of alchemists, hermeticists, and others of that ilk: "I have shown that Ptolemy luxuriates in using comparisons in a poetical or rhetorical way, since the things that he compares are not real things in the heavens" (as cited in Vickers, 1984, p. 153). He is equally critical of the Theosophist Fludd:

> One sees that Fludd takes his chief pleasure in incomprehensible picture puzzles of the reality, whereas I go forth from there, precisely to move into the bright light of knowledge the facts of nature which are veiled in darkness. The former is the subject of the chemist, followers of Hermes and Paracelsus, the latter, on the contrary, the task of the mathematician. (as cited in Caspar, 1993, pp. 292–293)

A letter to a colleague in 1608 makes it clear that Kepler believed both that analogy is heuristic, not deductive, and that to be worthwhile analogies must preserve interrelationships and causal structure:

> I too play with symbols, and have planned a little work, Geometric Cabala, which is about the Ideas of natural things in geometry; but I play in such a way that I do not forget that I am playing. For nothing is proved by symbols ... unless by sure reasons it can be demonstrated that they are not merely symbolic but are *descriptions of the ways in which the two things are connected and of the causes of this connexion* [italics added]. (as cited in Vickers, 1984, p. 155)

Analogy and Conceptual Change

We have established that Kepler used analogy intensively and that he meant by *analogy* roughly what we do. We now come to the crucial questions: To what extent did Kepler undergo conceptual change? Was analogy instrumental in this change? Some instances of the change of knowledge accomplished over Kepler's lifework are as follows:

1. The planetary system changed from one governed by mathematical law to one governed by physical causality. As noted by Gingerich (1993): "Copernicus gave the world a revolutionary helio*static* system, but Kepler made it into a heliocentric system. In Kepler's universe, the Sun has a fundamental physically motivated centrality that is essentially lacking in *De revolutionibus.* We have grown so accustomed to calling this the Copernican system that we usually forget than many of its attributes could better be called the Keplerian system" (p. 333).

2. Formerly, the planets' orbits were conceived of either as crystalline spheres containing the planets or as eternal circles traveled by planetary intelligences. Kepler came to see them as paths continually negotiated between the Sun and the planets. As Toulmin and Goodfield (1961) noted: "One cannot find before Kepler

any clear recognition that the heavenly motions called for an explanation in terms of a *continuously* acting physical force" (p. 201).

3. Formerly, celestial phenomena were considered completely separate from earthly physics. From the start, Kepler extended terrestrial knowledge to astronomical phenomena. Over the course of his work, he projected analogies from the domains of light, magnetism, balance scales, sailing, and the optics of lenses, among others.

4. Formerly, the paths of the planets were composed of perfect circles of uniform speed. As early as the *Mysterium,* Kepler gave up uniform speed. Over the next several years, Kepler also gave up on circularity, shifting to the belief that the planets move in ellipses with the Sun at one focus, faster when closer and slower when further. This was a far more radical change than most of us can today appreciate: "Before Kepler, circular motion was to the concept of a planet as 'tangibility' is to our concept of 'physical object'" (Hanson, 1958, p. 4).

5. Early in Kepler's work, he proposed the *anima motrix* as the "spirit" in the Sun that could move the planets. Later, he called it the *vis motrix* or *virtus motrix.* This change could be considered an ontological change, an instance of what Thagard (1992) called "branch jumping" from animate to inanimate. It may alternatively be better analyzed as akin to Wiser and Carey's (1983) "degree of heat"—a case of an anima–mechanistic notion that differentiated or specialized into a mechanical notion. In either case, it marked a shift toward a mechanistic notion of the influence from the Sun.

6. Early in Kepler's work, the planets (on the Stoic account) were, or possessed, intelligences (Barker, 1991). Kepler struggled with the notion of a planetary intelligence throughout his career. It was not merely a question of persuading others that an animate spirit was superfluous. The more fundamental issue was that Kepler himself had to find a way of thinking about the planets that constrained and motivated their lawful interactions, although assigning to them the minimal possible degree of sentience. Lacking any established notion of force, Kepler developed these ideas by gradually stripping away from the notion of "planetary intelligence" more and more of its specific properties. For example, he asked himself whether he could explain the fact that planets go faster when nearer the sun by granting them only the ability to "perceive" the Sun's diameter. Thus, the notion of "mind" underwent a kind of progressive abstraction. Indeed, Stephenson (1987) suggested that in many cases Kepler's speculations about celestial minds were really hypothetical analyses of abstract physical constraints.

How should we characterize the magnitude of these changes? The term *conceptual change* is sometimes used to refer to any significant change in conceptual structure. However, it is often useful to distinguish three grades of change (see Thagard, 1992, for a more detailed discussion of degrees of conceptual change). *Belief revision* is a change in facts believed. *Theory change* is a change in the global knowledge structure. Conceptual change, in some sense the most drastic, is a change in the fundamental concepts that compose the belief structure. Conceptual change thus requires at least locally nonalignable or incommensurable beliefs (Carey, 1985). Of the six changes mentioned previously regarding Kepler's lifework, we suggest that most if not all of them would qualify as theory change, and that Points 2, 5, and 6 have a good claim to be full-fledged changes of concepts.

Was analogy instrumental in these changes or merely a rhetorical device for conveying them? As mentioned earlier, the first evidence for this point is the intense, closely reasoned extended analogy passages in Kepler's writing (of which we had space to show only a small portion). In his 1621 annotations to the *Mysterium Cosmographicum* is more direct evidence that Kepler commented explicitly on the role of analogy in his knowledge revision process. In the original version, in 1596, he had argued that there was "a single moving soul [*motricem anima*] in the center of all the spheres, that is, in the Sun, and it impels each body more strongly in proportion to how near it is" (Kepler, 1596/1981, p. 199). In 1621, he wrote:

> If for the word "soul" [*Anima*] you substitute the word "force" [*Vim*], you have the very same principle on which the Celestial Physics is established. ... For once I believed that the cause which moves the planets was precisely a soul, as I was of course imbued with the doctrines of J. D. Scaliger on moving intelligences. But, when I pondered that this moving cause grows weaker with distance, and that the Sun's light also grows thinner with distance from the Sun, from that I concluded, that this force is something corporeal, that is, an emanation which a body emits, but an immaterial one. (Kepler, 1621/1969, p. 201)

Kepler Compared With Current Practice

One final, indirect argument for the position that analogy was instrumental in Kepler's changes of belief comes from Dunbar's (1994) observations of microbiology laboratories. His observations of the research process suggest that analogy plays a role in working scientists' online creative thinking. Dunbar's question is, of course, quite different from ours. He asked what makes for change of knowledge in a laboratory, whereas we are asking what makes for change of knowledge in an individual. However, his observations are valuable because they serve as a partial check on whether the historical retrospective account we have devised has any online plausibility. There are some striking commonalities. The microbiology laboratories that showed the most progress were those that used a large variety of analogies. Dunbar's detailed analyses of transcripts show that analogies are taken very seriously by the successful lab groups; they are extended and "pushed" in group discussions. Another interesting commonality is that Dunbar found that creativity is best fostered by multiple analogies, each treated quite analytically, and this accords with our conclusions from Kepler's works. Dunbar also found that a variety of base domains is useful and this too is characteristic of Kepler. Indeed, Kepler seems to have profited considerably from a comparison of the magnet and light analogs with each other as well as with the intended target domain of the motive power of the Sun.

There are also commonalities not directly related to analogy. Attention to inconsistencies is another factor Dunbar singled out in his analysis of creative laboratories. Kepler worried about inconsistencies and was driven by them to keep pushing old analogies and in some cases to reject them. However, we would amplify Dunbar's analysis slightly, in that we consider attention to inconsistencies a motivator for conceptual change, rather than (like analogy) a process leading to conceptual change.

There are also some interesting differences between Dunbar's (1994) observations and Kepler's behavior. First, by far the vast majority of the analogies Dunbar observed are close literal similarities (what he called local analogies), typically involving the same organism type or species, similar diseases, similar genetic materials, and so forth. Kepler did in fact use close analogs on many occasions. He tested his reasoning about the Sun and the planets by applying that same reasoning to the Earth and the Moon, which he regarded as a basically analogous system. He used analogies between the planets on many occasions profitably, notably the analogy between Mars and the Earth, which was instrumental in his computing of Mars's orbit. However, it should be noted that these analogies appear closer now than they did in 1625. Moreover, in contrast to the microbiologists, Kepler used many distant analogies. This stems in part from the different historical stages of the domains. Kepler was forming the new science of astrophysics, more or less in the absence of a usable physics. Distant analogies were in many cases his only option. There was no literal similarity to be had. In contrast, in the microbiology laboratories that Dunbar (1994) studied, the historical moment is one of a well-developed (but not yet fully explored) framework in which many close analogies exist that are likely to be extremely fruitful. Thus, we suspect that whether close analogies or far analogies are used depends in part on the historical context. Local analogies are useful for filling in an established framework, whereas distant analogies are used for creating a new framework.

Analogy and Business as Usual

Analogical reasoning does not always promote conceptual change. In fact, we believe analogy and similarity are most frequently used to retrieve and use prior cases from memory without significantly altering conceptual structure. Similarity-based access to long-term memory most often produces mundane literal similarity matches (Gentner et al., 1993; Reeves & Weisberg, 1994; Ross, 1989). Previous research has shown that people use prior cases or problems to conserve reasoning time when attempting to solve a novel problem (Bassok & Holyoak, 1989; Gick & Holyoak, 1980; Holyoak, Koh, & Nisbett, 1989; Novick & Holyoak, 1991; Novick & Tversky, 1987; Ross, 1987; Ross, Ryan, & Tenpenny, 1989). Case-based reasoning researchers have modeled this behavior with a variety of computer simulations (e.g., Birnbaum & Collins, 1989; Collins, 1989; Hammond, 1986, 1989; Kolodner, 1992, 1993; Kolodner & Simpson, 1989; Schank, 1982).

There is even evidence that analogy can sometimes inhibit conceptual change (Chi, Bassok, Lewis, Reimann, & Glaser, 1989; Chi & VanLehn, 1991). Chi et al. found that participants who were poor physics problem solvers were more likely than good physics problem solvers to refer back to worked out examples. Using analogy in this manner is characterized by making concrete matches, often local attribute matches, without matching higher order structure: for example, searching for the same term in base and target algebra problems. We have characterized this kind of analogizing as *analogy as recipe:* The analogist uses analogy to avoid hard thought, as when we fill out our tax form by cribbing from last years.' However, such uses contrast sharply with Kepler's kind of analogizing, which we can characterize as *analogy as X-ray.* This use of analogy is characterized by pursuing an alignment, noting differences, articulating common systems, and in general allowing the comparison to illuminate the topics. As Kepler's writings show, such analogies can promote deep conceptual change.

Creativity, Structure, and Conceptual Change

There is a common intuition that creative thinking is characterized by fuzzy concepts and shifting conceptual boundaries. This intuition has manifested itself in dissatisfaction with symbolic systems, which have been criticized as rigid, brittle, and unable to show transfer beyond the tasks for which they were designed. Indeed, on the face of it, ideas like "fluid representations" and "flexible processes" seem highly congenial to creative processing and conceptual change. Yet, we suggest that the true case, at least for scientific creativity, is closer to the opposite: Creativity is best realized with deeply structured representations that are relatively firm, but that admit limited, structurally guided alterations. Fluid, dynamic models may be appropriate for capturing the kind of gradual generalizations that occur across close similarity matches, as in learning to recognize handwriting; however, these kinds of changes are often recombinant shifts of small, anonymous subclusters. The shifting subclusters may fail to result in noticeable differences. In contrast, in structured representations the presence of higher order relational structure can permit rapid conceptual change between significantly different belief structures.

Of all the proposed mechanisms of learning—including accretion, tuning and compilation (Anderson, 1982), differentiation (Wiser & Carey, 1983), and generalization—analogy is the only one that offers the possibility of a self-generated large-scale transformation of knowledge in a concerted period. For example, SME, a system that thrives on structured representations, behaves in what may be considered to be a creative manner when it notices cross-dimensional structural matches, projects candidate inferences, infers skolomized entities and incrementally extends its mapping. Falkenhainer's PHINEAS, which extended SME with rerepresentation capabilities, went even further in this direction. Although these models are still a long way from the goal, and the right combination of fluidity and rigidity may still be in the offing, we suspect that the route to modeling creative conceptual change lies through, not around, structure.

Analogy's power to reveal common structure and to import structure from a well-articulated domain into a less coherent domain makes it the foremost instrument of major theory change. Our analysis of Kepler's writings reveals that analogy was indeed his "most Faithful Servant."

ACKNOWLEDGMENTS

This work was supported by National Science Foundation Grant BNS–87–20301 and Office of Naval Research Grant N00014–89–J1272. Ronald W. Ferguson received support from a Northwestern University Cognitive Science Fellowship. Björn Levidow was supported by a James S. McDonnell foundation postdoctoral fellowship.

REFERENCES

Aiton, E. J. (1976). Johannes Kepler in the light of recent research. *Historical Science, 14,* 77–100.
Anderson, J. R. (1982). Acquisition of cognitive skill. *Psychological Review, 89,* 369–406.
Barker, P. (1991). Stoic contributions to early modern science. In M. J. Osler (Ed.), *Atoms, pneuma, and tranquility: Epicurean and stoic themes in European thought* (pp. 135–154). Cambridge, MA: Cambridge University Press.
Barker, P. (1993). The optical theory of comets from Apian to Kepler. *Physis: Rivista Internzionale di Storia Della Scienza, 30*(1), 1–25.
Barker, P., & Goldstein, B. R. (1994). Distance and velocity in Kepler's astronomy. *Annals of Science, 51,* 59–73.
Bassok, M. (1990). Transfer of domain-specific problem-solving procedures. *Journal of Experimental Psychology: Learning, Memory, and Cognition, 16,* 522–533.
Bassok, M., & Holyoak, K. J. (1989). Interdomain transfer between isomorphic topics in algebra and physics. *Journal of Experimental Psychology: Learning, Memory, and Cognition, 15,* 153–166.
Baumgardt, C. (1952). *Johannes Kepler: Life and letters.* London: Victor Gollancz.
Birnbaum, L., & Collins, G. (1989). Remindings and engineering design themes: A case study in indexing vocabulary. In *Proceedings of the Case-Based Reasoning Workshop* (pp. 47–51). San Mateo, CA: Kaufmann.
Boronat, C., & Gentner, D. (1996). *Metaphors are (sometimes) processed as generative domain mappings.* Unpublished manuscript.

Bowdle, B. F., & Gentner, D. (1996). *Informativity and asymmetry in comparisons.* Unpublished manuscript.

Brown, J. S., Collins, A., & Duguid, P. (1989). Situated cognition and the culture of learning. *Educational Researcher, 18,* 32–42.

Burstein, M. H. (1986). Concept formation by incremental analogical reasoning and debugging. In R. S. Michalski, J. G. Carbonell, & T. M. Mitchell (Eds.), *Machine learning: An artificial intelligence approach* (Vol. 2, pp. 351–378). Los Altos, CA: Kaufmann.

Butterfield, H. (1957). *The origins of modern science 1300–1800.* New York: Free Press.

Carey, S. (1985). *Conceptual change in childhood.* Cambridge, MA: MIT Press.

Casper, M. (1993). *Kepler* (C. D. Hellman, Trans.). New York: Dover.

Catrambone, R., & Holyoak, K. J. (1989). Overcoming contextual limitations on problem-solving transfer. *Journal of Experimental Psychology: Learning, Memory, & Cognition, 15,* 1147–1156.

Chi, M. T. H., Bassok, M., Lewis, M. W., Reimann, P., & Glaser, R. (1989). Self-explanations: How students use examples in learning to solve problems. *Cognitive Science, 13,* 145–182.

Chi, M. T., & VanLehn, K. A. (1991). The content of physics self-explanations. *Journal of the Learning Sciences, 1,* 69–105.

Clement, C. A., & Gentner, D. (1991). Systematicity as a selection constraint in analogical mapping. *Cognitive Science, 15,* 89–132.

Collins, G. (1989). Plan adaptation: A transformational approach. In *Proceedings of the Case-Based Reasoning Workshop* (pp. 90–93). San Mateo, CA: Kaufmann.

Darden, L. (1992). Strategies for anomaly resolution. In R. N. Giere (Ed.), *Cognitive models of science* (pp. 251–273). Minneapolis: University of Minnesota Press.

Dunbar, K. (1994). Scientific discovery heuristics: How current day scientists generate new hypotheses and make scientific discoveries. In A. Ram & K. Eislet (Eds.), *Proceedings of the Sixteenth Annual Conference of the Cognitive Science Society* (pp. 985–986). Hillsdale, NJ: Lawrence Erlbaum Associates, Inc.

Elio, R., & Anderson, J. R. (1981). The effect of category generalizations and instance similarity on schema abstraction. *Journal of Experimental Psychology: Human Learning and Memory, 7,* 397–417.

Elio, R., & Anderson, J. R. (1984). The effects of information order and learning mode on schema abstraction. *Memory & Cognition, 12,* 20–30.

Falkenhainer, B. (1990). A unified approach to explanation and theory formation. In J. Shrager & P. Langley (Eds.), *Computational models of scientific discovery and theory formation* (pp. 157–196). San Mateo, CA: Kaufmann.

Falkenhainer, B., Forbus, K. D., & Gentner, D. (1986). The structure-mapping engine. In *Proceedings of the Fifth National Conference on Artificial Intelligence* (pp. 272–277). Philadelphia: Kaufmann.

Falkenhainer, B., Forbus, K. D., & Gentner, D. (1989). The structure-mapping engine: An algorithm and examples. *Artificial Intelligence, 41,* 1–63.

Forbus, K. D. (1984). Qualitative process theory. *Journal of Artificial Intelligence, 24,* 85–168.

Forbus, K. D. (1990). Qualitative physics: Past present and future. In D. S. Weld & J. de Kleer (Eds.), *Readings in qualitative reasoning about physical systems* (pp. 11–39). San Mateo, CA: Kaufmann.

Forbus, K., Ferguson, R., & Gentner, D. (1994). Incremental structure-mapping. In A. Ram & K. Eislet (Eds.), *Proceedings of the Sixteenth Annual Conference of the Cognitive Science Society* (pp. 313–318). Hillsdale, NJ: Lawrence Erlbaum Associates, Inc.

Forbus, K. D., & Gentner, D. (1986). Learning physical domains: Toward a theoretical framework. In R. S. Michalski, J. G. Carbonell, & T. M. Mitchell (Eds.), *Machine learning: An artificial intelligence approach* (pp. 311–348). Los Altos, CA: Kaufmann.

Forbus, K. D., & Gentner, D. (1989). Structural evaluation of analogies: What counts? In *Proceedings of the Eleventh Annual Conference of the Cognitive Science Society* (pp. 314–348). Hillsdale, NJ: Lawrence Erlbaum Associates, Inc.

Forbus, K. D., Gentner, D., & Law, K. (1995). MAC/FAC: A model of similarity-based retrieval. *Cognitive Science, 19,* 141–205.

Forbus, K. D., & Oblinger, D. (1990). Making SME greedy and pragmatic. In *Proceedings of the Twelfth Annual Conference of the Cognitive Science Society* (pp. 61–68). Hillsdale, NJ: Lawrence Erlbaum Associates, Inc.

Gentner, D. (1982). Are scientific analogies metaphors? In D. S. Miall (Ed.), *Metaphor: Problems and perspectives* (pp. 106–132). Brighton, England: Harvester.

Gentner, D. (1983). Structure-mapping: A theoretical framework for analogy. *Cognitive Science, 7,* 155–170.

Gentner, D. (1988). Metaphor as structure mapping: The relational shift. *Child Development, 59,* 47–59.

Gentner, D. (1989). The mechanisms of analogical learning. In S. Vosniadou & A. Ortony (Eds.), *Similarity and analogical reasoning* (pp. 199–241). Cambridge, England: Cambridge University Press.

Gentner, D., & Boronat, C. B. (1992). *Metaphors as mapping.* Paper presented at the Workshop on Metaphor, Tel Aviv, Israel.

Gentner, D., & Bowdle, B. (1994). The coherence imbalance hypothesis: A functional approach to asymmetry in comparison. In A. Ram & K. Eislet (Eds.), *Proceedings of the Sixteenth Annual Conference of the Cognitive Science Society* (pp. 351–356). Hillsdale, NJ: Lawrence Erlbaum Associates, Inc.

Gentner, D., & Clement, C. (1988). Evidence for relational selectivity in the interpretation of analogy and metaphor. In G. H. Bower (Ed.), *The psychology of learning and motivation, advances in research and theory* (pp. 307–358). New York: Academic.

Gentner, D., & Gentner, D. R. (1983). Flowing waters or teeming crowds: Mental models of electricity. In D. Gentner & A. Stevens (Eds.), *Mental models* (pp. 99–129). Hillsdale, NJ: Lawrence Erlbaum Associates, Inc.

Gentner, D., & Imai, M. (1995). A further examination of the shape bias in early word learning. In *Proceedings of the Twenty-Sixth Annual Child Language Research Forum* (pp. 167–176). Stanford, CA: Center for the Study of Language and Information.

Gentner, D., & Jeziorski, M. (1993). The shift from metaphor to analogy in Western science. In A. Ortony (Ed.), *Metaphor and thought* (pp. 447–480). Cambridge, England: Cambridge University Press.

Gentner, D., & Markman, A. B. (1993). Analogy—Watershed or Waterloo? Structural alignment and the development of connectionist models of cognition. In S. J. Hanson, J. D. Cowan, & C. L. Giles (Eds.), *Advances in neural information processing systems* (Vol. 5, pp. 855–862). San Mateo, CA: Kauffman.

Gentner, D., & Markman, A. B. (1994). Structural alignment in comparison: No difference without similarity. *Psychological Science, 5,* 152–158.

Gentner, D., & Markman, A. B. (in press). Structure-mapping in analogy and similarity. *American Psychologist.*

Gentner, D., & Rattermann, J. J. (1991). Language and the career of similarity. In S. A. Gelman & J. P. Byrnes (Eds.), *Perspectives on language and thought: Interrelations in development* (pp. 225–277). Cambridge, England: Cambridge University Press.

Gentner, D., Rattermann, M. J., & Forbus, K. D. (1993). The roles of similarity in transfer: Separating retrievability from inferential soundness. *Cognitive Psychology, 25,* 524–575.

Gentner, D., Rattermann, M. J., Markman, A. B., & Kotovsky, L. (1995). Two forces in the development of relational similarity. In T. J. Simon & G. S. Halford (Eds.), *Developing cognitive competence: New approaches to process modeling* (pp. 263–313). Hillsdale, NJ: Lawrence Erlbaum Associates, Inc.

Gentner, D., & Wolff, P. (in press). Metaphor and knowledge change. In A. Kasher & V. Shen (Eds.), *Cognitive aspects of metaphor: Structure, comprehension and use.*

Gick, M. L., & Holyoak, K. J. (1980). Analogical problem solving. *Cognitive Psychology, 12,* 306–355.

Gick, M. L., & Holyoak, K. J. (1983). Schema induction and analogical transfer. *Cognitive Psychology, 15,* 1–38.

Gingerich, O. (1993). *The eye of heaven.* New York: The American Institute of Physics.

Glashow, S. L. (1980). Towards a unified theory: Threads in a tapestry. *Science, 210,* 1319–1323.

Halford, G. S. (1993). *Children's understanding. The development of mental models.* Hillsdale, NJ: Lawrence Erlbaum Associates, Inc.

Hammond, K. J. (1986). CHEF: A model of case-based planning. In *Proceedings of the Fifth National Conference on Artificial Intelligence* (pp. 267–271). Philadelphia: Kaufmann.

Hammond, K. J. (1989). *Case-based planning: Viewing planning as a memory task.* Boston: Academic.

Hanson, N. R. (1958). *Patterns of discovery; an inquiry into the conceptual foundations of science.* Cambridge, England: Cambridge University Press.

Holton, G. (1973). *Thematic origins of scientific thought.* Cambridge, MA: Harvard University Press.

Holyoak, K. J., Junn, E. N., & Billman, D. O. (1984). Development of analogical problem-solving skill. *Child Development, 55,* 2042–2055.

Holyoak, K. J., Koh, K., & Nisbett, R. E. (1989). A theory of conditioning: Inductive learning within rule-based default hierarchies. *Psychological Review, 96,* 315–340.

Holyoak, K. J., & Thagard, P. R. (1989). Analogical mapping by constraint satisfaction. *Cognitive Science, 13,* 295–355.

Kass, A. (1994). Tweaker: Adapting old explanations to new situations. In R. Schank, A. Kass, & C. K. Riesbeck (Eds.), *Inside case-based explanation* (pp. 263–295). Hillsdale, NJ: Lawrence Erlbaum Associates, Inc.

Keane, M. T. (1988). Analogical mechanisms. *Artificial Intelligence Review, 2,* 229–250.

Keane, M. T. G. (1990). Incremental analogizing: Theory and model. In K. J. Gilhooly, M. T. G. Keane, R. H. Logie, & G. Erdos (Eds.), *Lines of thinking.* Chichester, England: Wiley.

Kepler, J. (1952). Harmonice mundi (C. G. Wallis, Trans.). In *Great books of the Western world* (Vol. 16, pp. 1005–1085). Chicago. (Original work published 1619)

Kepler, J. (1969). *Epitome of Copernican astronomy* (C. G. Wallis, Trans.). New York: Kraus Reprint. (Original work published 1621)

Kepler, J. (1981). *Mysterium cosmographicum I, II* (A. M. Duncan, Trans.). (2nd ed.). New York: Abaris Books. (Original work published 1596)

Kepler, J. (1992). *New astronomy* (W. Donahue, Trans.). Cambridge, England: Cambridge University Press. (Original work published 1609)

Koestler, A. (1963). *The sleepwalkers.* New York: Grosset & Dunlap.

Kolodner, J. L. (1992). An introduction to case-based reasoning. *Artificial Intelligence Review, 6,* 3–34.

Kolodner, J. L. (1993). *Case-based reasoning.* San Mateo, CA: Kaufmann.

Kolodner, J. L., & Simpson, R. L. (1989). The MEDIATOR: Analysis of an early case-based problem solver. *Cognitive Science, 13,* 507–549.

Kotovsky, L., & Gentner, D. (in press). Comparison and categorization in the development of relational similarity. *Child Development.*

Koyre, A. (1973). *The astronomical revolution: Copernicus, Kepler, Borelli* (R. E. W. Maddison, Trans.). Ithaca, NY: Cornell University Press. (Original work published 1892)

Kuhn, T. S. (1957). *The Copernican revolution: Planetary astronomy in the development of Western thought.* Cambridge, MA: Harvard University Press.

Langley, P., Bradshaw, G. L., & Simon, H. A. (1983). Rediscovering chemistry with the BACON system. In R. S. Michalski, J. G. Carbonell, & T. M. Mitchell (Eds.), *Machine learning: An artificial intelligence approach* (pp. 307–329). Los Altos, CA: Kaufmann.

Layzer, D. (1984). *Constructing the universe.* New York: Scientific American.

Markman, A. B. (1996). *Constraints on analogical inference.* Unpublished manuscript.

Markman, A. B., & Gentner, D. (1993a). Splitting the differences: A structural alignment view of similarity. *Journal of Memory and Language, 32,* 517–535.

Markman, A. B., & Gentner, D. (1993b). Structural alignment during similarity comparisons. *Cognitive Psychology, 25,* 431–467.

Markman, A. B., & Gentner, D. (1996). Commonalities and differences in similarity comparisons. *Memory and Cognition, 24,* 235–249.

Markman, A. B., & Gentner, D. (in press). The effects of alignability on memory storage. *Psychological Science.*

Mason, S. F. (1962). *A history of the sciences.* New York: Macmillan.

Medin, D. L., Goldstone, R. L., & Gentner, D. (1993). Respects for similarity. *Psychological Review, 100,* 254–278.

Medin, D. L., & Ross, B. H. (1989). The specific character of abstract thought: Categorization, problem-solving, and induction. In R. J. Sternberg (Ed.), *Advances in the psychology of human intelligence* (Vol. 5, pp. 189–223). Hillsdale, NJ: Lawrence Erlbaum Associates, Inc.

Miller, G. A. (1979). Images and models, similes and metaphors. In A. Ortony (Ed.), *Metaphor and thought* (pp. 202–250). Cambridge, England: Cambridge University Press.

Nersessian, N. J. (1985). Faraday's field concept. In D. Gooding & F. James (Eds.), *Faraday rediscovered* (pp. 175–187). London: Macmillan.

Nersessian, N. J. (1986). A cognitive-historical approach to meaning in scientific theories. In N. J. Nersessian (Ed.), *The process of science: Contemporary philosophical approaches to understanding scientific practice.* Dordrecht, The Netherlands: Martinus Nijhoff.

Nersessian, N. J. (1992). How do scientists think? Capturing the dynamics of conceptual change in science. In R. N. Giere & H. Feigl (Eds.), *Minnesota studies in the philosophy of science* (pp. 3–44). Minneapolis: University of Minnesota Press.

Nersessian, N. J., & Resnick, L. B. (1989). Comparing historical and intuitive explanations of motion: Does "naive physics" have a structure? In *Proceedings of the Eleventh Annual Conference of the Cognitive Science Society* (pp. 412–420). Hillsdale, NJ: Lawrence Erlbaum Associates, Inc.

Novick, L. R., & Holyoak, K. J. (1991). Mathematical problem solving by analogy. *Journal of Experimental Psychology: Learning, Memory, & Cognition, 17,* 398–415.

Novick, L. R., & Tversky, B. (1987). Cognitive constraints on ordering operations: The case of geometric analogies. *Journal of Experimental Psychology: General, 116,* 50–67.

Oppenheimer, R. (1956). Analogy in science. *American Psychologist, 11,* 127–135.

Ortony, A. (1979). Beyond literal similarity. *Psychological Review, 86,* 161–180.

Ortony, A., Vondruska, R. J., Foss, M. A., & Jones, L. E. (1985). Salience, similes, and the asymmetry of similarity. *Journal of Memory and Language, 24,* 569–594.

Ranney, M., & Thagard, P. (1988). Explanatory coherence and belief revision in naive physics. In *Proceedings of the Tenth Annual Conference of the Cognitive Science Society* (pp. 426–432). Hillsdale, NJ: Lawrence Erlbaum Associates, Inc.

Reeves, L. M., & Weisberg, R. W. (1994). The role of content and abstract information in analogical transfer. *Psychological Bulletin, 115,* 381–400.

Ross, B. H. (1984). Remindings and their effects in learning a cognitive skill. *Cognitive Psychology, 16,* 371–416.

Ross, B. H. (1987). This is like that: The use of earlier problems and the separation of similarity effects. *Journal of Experimental Psychology: Learning, Memory, & Cognition, 13,* 629–639.

Ross, B. H. (1989). Distinguishing types of superficial similarities: Different effects on the access and use of earlier examples. *Journal of Experimental Psychology: Learning, Memory, and Cognition, 15,* 456–468.

Ross, B. H., Ryan, W. J., & Tenpenny, P. L. (1989). The access of relevant information for solving problems. *Memory & Cognition, 17,* 639–651.

Sambursky, S. (1975). *Physical thought from the presocratics to the quantum physicists: An anthology.* New York: Pica.

Schank, R. (1982). *Dynamic memory: A theory of reminding and learning in computers and people.* Cambridge, MA: Cambridge University Press.

Skorstad, J., Gentner, D., & Medin, D. (1988). Abstraction processes during concept learning: A structural view. In *Proceedings of the Tenth Annual Conference of the Cognitive Science Society* (pp. 419–425). Hillsdale, NJ: Lawrence Erlbaum Associates, Inc.

Spellman, B. A., & Holyoak, K. J. (1993). An inhibitory mechanism for goal-directed analogical mapping. In *Proceedings of the Fifteenth Annual Conference of the Cognitive Science Society* (pp. 947–952). Hillsdale, NJ: Lawrence Erlbaum Associates, Inc.

Spiro, R. J., Feltovich, P. J., Coulson, R. L., & Anderson, D. K. (1989). Multiple analogies for complex concepts: Antidotes for analogy-induced misconception in advanced knowledge acquisition. In S. Vosniadou & A. Ortony (Eds.), *Similarity and analogical reasoning* (pp. 498–531). New York: Cambridge University Press.

Stephenson, B. (1994a). *Kepler's physical astronomy.* Princeton, NJ: Princeton University Press.

Stephenson, B. (1994b). *The music of the heavens.* Princeton, NJ: Princeton University Press.

Thagard, P. (1989). Explanatory coherence. *Behavioral and Brain Sciences, 12,* 435–502.

Thagard, P. (1992). *Conceptual revolutions.* Princeton, NJ: Princeton University Press.

Toulmin, S., & Goodfield, J. (1961). *The fabric of the heavens.* New York: Harper.

Tourangeau, R., & Rips, L. (1991). Interpreting and evaluating metaphors. *Journal of Memory and Language, 30,* 452–472.

Tweney, R. D. (1983, June). *Cognitive psychology and the analysis of science: Michael Faraday and the uses of experiment.* Paper presented at the ninth annual meeting of the Society for Philosophy and Psychology, Wellesley College, Wellesley, MA.

Vickers, B. (1984). Analogy versus identity: The rejection of occult symbolism, 1580–1680. In B. Vickers (Ed.), *Occult and scientific mentalities in the Renaissance* (pp. 95–163). Cambridge, England: Cambridge University Press.

Winston, P. H. (1980). Learning and reasoning by analogy. *Communications of the ACM, 23,* 689–703.

Wiser, M., & Carey, S. (1983). When heat and temperature were one. In D. Gentner & A. L. Stevens (Eds.), *Mental models* (pp. 267–297). Hillsdale, NJ: Lawrence Erlbaum Associates, Inc.

THE JOURNAL OF THE LEARNING SCIENCES, 6(1), 41–60
Copyright © 1997, Lawrence Erlbaum Associates, Inc.

Conceptual Change and Wine Expertise

Gregg E. A. Solomon

Department of Brain and Cognitive Sciences
Massachusetts Institute of Technology

Two studies explore conceptual change in the acquisition of wine expertise. In Experiment 1, tasters described a set of wines. Experts described the wines using more specific features than did intermediates, who, in turn, used more specific features than did novices. Specificity in describing wines was not related to discrimination performance on a psychophysical test. A regression analysis indicated that the features identified by the expert as well as those identified by the nonexpert tasters covaried with grape type, such that wines of the same grape were described more similarly than were wines of different grapes. In Experiment 2, the same tasters sorted the wines into clusters. Experts, unlike nonexperts, tended to sort the wines explicitly by grape type. Moreover, the features of the wines (described by the tasters in Experiment 1) covaried significantly better by the experts' clusters than they did by the nonexperts' clusters. Indeed, the features identified by the nonexperts covaried significantly worse when the wines were clustered by their own sortings than they did when the wines were clustered by actual grape type. It is suggested that the acquisition of wine expertise, a domain that is at once conceptual and perceptual, entails not only a greater differentiation of features but also a restructuring of the explicit schemes of classification.

Once we grant that there are such things as experts and that they are, within their worlds, different from novices, we are led to ask just how profoundly different they are. Might they have undergone the kind of conceptual change described by students of the history of science and conceptual development (Carey, 1988, 1991; Chi, Hutchinson, & Robin, 1989; Kitcher, 1988; Kuhn, 1970, 1977; Nersessian, 1992)? Wine tasting is a domain particularly suited to such study, for the language of wine experts hints at a conceptual organization not immediately obvious to novices. Certainly, much has been made of the opacity of expert wine talk. Expert and novice

---

Requests for reprints should be sent to Gregg E. A. Solomon, Department of Brain and Cognitive Sciences, E10–044, Massachusetts Institute of Technology, 79 Amherst Street, Cambridge, MA 02142.

wine tasters may even constitute linguistic communities, with the language of one community not completely translatable into the language of the other. Differences in how experts and novices describe wines may reflect a particular aspect of conceptual change discussed by Kuhn (1977), Kitcher (1988), and Carey (1988, 1991): Even those concepts that are shared by two groups may be understood in different relations to other concepts. For evidence of this, let us look to classification—a very basic kind of relation judgment.

In classifying, we judge exemplars of a class to be, at some level, identical. If we take a class to entail a set of features, weighted in importance according to some metric (whether theoretical in nature or due to characteristics of processing), then we can infer that those objects classified together are similar on that set of salient features. In classifying, we imply that metric by which similarity is to be assessed and by which the class is defined. Kitcher (1988) discussed conceptual change in the history of science as a reordering of which concepts in a field are considered fundamental and which are derivative. Conceptual change in the acquisition of expertise may then be manifested as a reweighting of the features considered salient in determining or characterizing membership in a class, but a reweighting that reflects a different causal understanding of the domain.

It may well be that experts and novices know the world similarly, carving it up and understanding the relations of its parts in roughly the same way. Experts may differentiate more finely within novice classes; a given class may be separated into subsets, but the distinctions among the grosser classes may still be preserved as would the bases underlying judgments of similarity. Alternatively, it may be that experts know and classify in different, not merely more differentiated, ways. Expert and novice conceptual systems may be incommensurable (Carey, 1991; Kuhn, 1983). By this reasoning, the acquisition of expertise would entail a restructuring of the grosser classes distinguished by novices and a restructuring of the conceptual framework within which such classifications and understandings of feature saliences are embedded. The overarching questions are these: Do experts and novices describe wines using similar features (if at different levels of specificity), and do they understand these features to determine similar systems of classification?

Categorization is, of course, an essential act of mentation, allowing us to make inferences about novel aspects of the world. Among wine tasters, the ability to make more differentiated classification judgments would be of most advantage if wines were grouped not only because of social convention but also because the grouping captured something about how features are perceived in the world. Rosch and Mervis (1975) noted that we distinguish among categories on the basis of correlated properties. Moreover, Rosch, Mervis, Gray, Johnson, and Boyes-Braem (1976) claimed that features do not vary continuously in the perceived world but covary by classes of objects. Berlin (1978, 1981) similarly asserted that folk taxonomic divisions of the world correspond to gross disjunctions in morphological features. Malt and Smith (1984), on showing that there are correlated clusters of properties within basic level categories, posited that experts further divide categories in ways that maintain those clusters of properties. It follows that, with knowledge of more specific categories, tasters could take advantage of these purportedly correlated features and, guided by inference from more obvious features, search the perceptual array splashing across their palates for less obvious features. For example, when tasting a cabernet sauvignon, an expert may search for notes of bell pepper, a feature typical of wines of that grape.

One may argue that, because nature appears to be carved at certain joints, and our cognitive processes function so as best to take advantage of that order, experts and novices will differ only in the degree of specificity (and perhaps the accuracy) of their judgments. Indeed, Gibson and Gibson (1955) reasoned that the acquisition of wine expertise is largely a process of selective attention whereby tasters come to make distinctions within previously undifferentiated properties and classes of wines.

> The gentleman who is discriminating about his wine shows a high specificity of perception, whereas the crude fellow who is not shows a low specificity. A whole class of chemically different fluids is equivalent for the latter individual; he cannot tell the difference between a claret, burgundy, and chianti; his perceptions are relatively undifferentiated. ... If he is a genuine connoisseur and not a fake ... he can consistently apply nouns to the different fluids of a class and he can apply adjectives to the differences between the fluids. (Gibson & Gibson, 1955, p. 35)

The association of expertise with increased differentiation of features and classes has been noted in a range of domains from chick sexing to tree naming to bird, dog, and fish classification (Biederman & Shiffrar, 1987; Dougherty, 1978; Lunn, 1948; Tanaka & Taylor, 1991).

Rooted in perception, wine classification may follow along lines laid down by the predispositions of our gustatory and olfactory sense systems. Animal studies certainly suggest that generalization and discrimination learning can be supported (and impeded) by specific predispositions (Gallistel, Brown, Carey, Gelman, & Keil, 1991). One can imagine the evolutionary advantage conveyed by a predisposition in humans to identify some foods or fluids as, for example, sweet (because they are likely to be ripe and edible), sour (because they may be unripe), or bitter (because they may be poisonous). Given the perceptual nature of wine tasting, this line of argument would seem to imply that differences in how tasters classify wines may be more a question of whether experts and nonexperts are equally able to recognize given features than a question of how salient they consider those features to be. Experts and novices may describe and classify wines at different levels of specificity but within the same general organization of classes.

In this article, I pursue the possibility that experts and novices describe and classify wines in manners consistent with different conceptual organizations. I do not ask so much whether the specificity with which experts describe wines differs from that of novices. That much has been established (Lawless, 1984; Lehrer, 1983;

Solomon, 1990). Rather, I ask whether the manner of classification implied by those descriptions differs. Although the learning of more specific features may well proceed by perceptual learning, as described by Gibson (1966), experts may yet differ from novices in the conceptual importance they attach even to those features that are perceived and described by novices. Experts and novices may base their classification judgments on perceivable features in nonarbitrary ways but, as Lakoff (1986) emphasized, that is not to say that those features need determine a single scheme of classification. The same set of features may be weighted in such ways as to indicate different classes of wines for experts than for novices. Even if experts do make more class distinctions among wines, novices may judge two particular wines to fall in different classes, although experts may judge them to fall into the same class. Experts and novices may therefore differ in how they understand features to covary by class and, most important, in what that covariation means.

Different knowledge of how features are interrelated has been implicated in expert performance in other domains. Chess masters, for example, show a recall advantage over novices that is related to their different sense of how pieces cluster (Chase & Simon, 1973; de Groot, 1965). They apprehend individual chess pieces as members of thematically related arrays, as chunks of attack and defense. Chi, Feltovich, and Glaser (1981) also demonstrated the importance of conceptual organization to expert performance. Chi et al. reported that expert physicists use their knowledge of underlying, principled physical laws as a basis for categorizing physics problems, whereas novices categorized on the basis of superficial charac-teristics. Experts and novices understand physics from within different conceptual frameworks.

Chi and Koeske (1983) found that a child who was expert in a specific domain, dinosaurs, had a more integrated and cohesive organization of his knowledge about a set of more familiar dinosaurs than about a set of less familiar dinosaurs. Through a series of tasks, including attribute listing and sorting, the researchers represented the child's knowledge in terms of a semantic network with instances of dinosaurs, their attributes, and associations among them. The more familiar dinosaurs were represented with a greater number of attributes and associations among them. Moreover, they found that the child showed superior performance on memory tasks with the more highly structured set of dinosaurs than with the less structured set. Gobbo and Chi (1986) extended these results to explain differences among children, finding that those children who were dinosaur experts showed evidence of more integrated and cohesive knowledge about dinosaurs than did those who were novices. Chi et al. (1989) further pointed out that the novices were more apt to sort dinosaurs into groups on the basis of more explicit "surface" features (e.g., shape of leg), whereas the experts were more apt to base their sortings on "deeper" implicit features (e.g., diet). They suggested that the novices sorted the dinosaurs on an ad hoc basis, whereas the expert sortings appeared to reflect their utilization of a preexisting representation of a family structure or classification schema. Chi et al. interpreted their findings as supporting the notion that novices can undergo a conceptual change in acquiring expertise, such that there is a restructuring of their domain-specific knowledge. They suggested that with learning children come to recognize the covariation among features in the domain and that the children's knowledge of the domain is then restructured so as to capture those regularities that exist among dinosaurs.

Extending the implications of these studies to so seemingly perceptually driven a domain as wine tasting raises interesting theoretical (and empirical) possibilities. As they gain in expertise, wine tasters may come to notice regularities in wines, and the manner in which they make classification judgments may change to capture those regularities. However, one implication of the perceptual nature of wine tasting is that even if novices were found to classify on an ad hoc basis, and so fail to capture featural regularities, it would not be clear whether they did so because they were unable to identify the features that covary by class, or whether they were able to identify the relevant features but failed to appreciate their covariation and so failed to classify the wines accordingly. It is, in part, an empirical question.

These studies are, therefore, an initial exploration of two interrelated lines of inquiry: First, whether novices as well as experts identify features that covary among wines, and second, whether experts and novices both classify wines in manners that capture a regularity in nature and, if they do, whether they capture the same regularity. In Experiment 1, an indirect method was used to assess tasters' implicit appreciation of a regularity in the wine world. Tasters first described a set of wines. The similarity of the wines was determined by correlating the described features. We could then look to whether the featural similarities of these wines corresponded to an obvious division in the natural world: grape type. Wine is, after all, well-bred grape juice, and most respected books surveying wines are organized either by grape type alone or by region and grape type (e.g., Robinson, 1986). In many countries, labeling a wine by grape is even governed by law, suggesting that this means of division has psychological weight.

In Experiment 2, the tasters explicitly sorted the wines into classes, gave explanations for their groupings, and subsequently were debriefed as to their beliefs about what causes a wine to have the features it does. I could then assess whether experts and novices differed in their systems of classification and whether those classes corresponded to grape type. Furthermore, by comparing the degree to which the wines sorted together in Experiment 2 were described more similarly in Experiment 1, I could assess the extent to which tasters recognized a structure implicit in their own descriptions. Conceptual change in the acquisition of wine expertise would be manifested not only as a difference in how experts and novices sort wines but also in how they explain those sortings. We would expect experts and novices to have different senses of which attributes are fundamental causal features in wines and which are derivative.

Participants also took part in a preliminary psychophysical task to determine whether there were systematic differences among them in gross perceptual acuity. The experiments were conducted in intervals of approximately 1 week.

EXPERIMENT 1: WINE DESCRIPTIONS

Experiment 1 explored how possible differences between expert, intermediate, and novice tasters' understandings of the wine world may be manifested in their descriptions of wines. Tasters at an intermediate level of expertise were included in the studies in the hope that their performance may shed light on the acquisition of expertise. The tasters were presented with a set lexicon from which to choose their terms. Research among odor profilers (Chastrette, Elmouaffek, & Sauvegrain, 1988; Lawless, 1988) suggests that the tasters would be apt to list the features of the wines in a more comprehensive manner when checking terms off a list than when left to invoke their own terms. Most important, because the set was finite, the wine descriptions could be correlated on the basis of those features not chosen as well as those chosen. The descriptions could then be analyzed to determine whether experts, intermediates, and novices identified features such that they covaried similarly by grape type. Finally, the set lexicon also provided a basis for testing the common assumption that experts are more apt to perceive and describe wines with more specific features.

Method

Participants.   There were 28 volunteer participants in the experiments, 11 novices, 9 intermediates, and 8 experts, ranging in age from 22 to approximately 50 years old. Participants were considered novices on the basis of a questionnaire assessing their degree of experience with wine (see Appendix A). They had little formal wine-tasting experience and were infrequent wine drinkers. Participants deemed experts were or had been professionally engaged in the wine industry. They included wholesale buyers, retail managers, sommeliers, wine educators, and writers. Participants were designated intermediates if they were not novices and were endeavoring, formally or informally, to increase their knowledge about wine but had never been professionally involved in the industry. Most intermediates either worked in the food industry or were studying to do so. They did not consider themselves to be experts.

Participants first took part in a preliminary psychophysical task known as the Triangle Test (Amerine & Roessler, 1983) to determine whether gross differences existed in the tasters' abilities to discriminate among wines.[1] The test neither revealed significant differences between the experts, intermediates, and novices in their abilities to distinguish among the wines (even though the experts were not at ceiling) nor did their performances on this task correlate significantly with their performances on subsequent tasks.

Stimuli.   The stimuli for Experiments 1 and 2 consisted of 10 moderately priced white wines (see Appendix C). Pilot testing indicated that 10 wines were the most that participants could reasonably be expected to taste at one sitting. (Although several experts claimed that they could have tasted many more wines without any diminution in their abilities, the novices were not so sanguine.) The wines were selected, with the help of local wine consultants, to provide a range in the extent to which they may be considered typical of grape or region. Five chardonnays were chosen (one from Chablis in France, two from the Napa Valley, one from Santa Barbara, and one from the Hunter Valley in Australia), two sauvignon blancs (one a fumé blanc from California and the other a Sancerre from France), two pinot gris (one from Alsace in France and one from Friuli in Italy, where the grape is known as pinot grigio), and one gewürztraminer (from Alsace).

The 10 wines were served blind, in coded 8-oz wine glasses, with the order of the glasses from left to right balanced across participants. Each glass contained about 2 oz of wine. The glasses were washed in very hot water without soap (to reduce the risk of off odors). The wines were tasted after having been allowed to breathe for at least 10 min and were tasted at most 1½ hr after opening. Wines can be expected to change over time (and contribute noise to the data). Therefore, after each pouring, the bottles were sealed using a Vacu-vin vacuum pump.

---

[1]Four very similar, relatively cheap white Bordeaux wines served as stimuli for the task (see Appendix B). They were not the same wines used in Experiments 1 and 2 because pilot testing indicated that those 10 wines were simply too different and would have resulted in a ceiling effect. The four wines used in this experiment were selected to make the task as difficult as possible to exaggerate potential differences in discrimination. Tasters were presented with three glasses of wine, two of which contained the same wine from the same bottle. They attempted to indicate which of the three glasses contained the odd wine. After a participant had selected one of the wines, the three glasses were moved behind a screen and three more were presented. Participants performed this task eight times. Every wine was presented at least once with every other wine and the order of presentation was balanced across participants. To reduce the possibility of visual cues, the lights were dimmed and participants wore dark sunglasses during the tasting. Each participant had a 1 in 3 chance of guessing correctly on any given trial. Chance performance over the eight trials would likely yield 2.67 correct choices. A one-way analysis of variance indicated that the novice group mean of 3.73, the intermediate group mean of 4.00, and the expert group mean of 4.57 correct choices were not significantly different.

Procedure.   Participants tasted the wines and then spat into buckets. They were provided with water and baguettes to cleanse their palates between wines. Each experiment lasted from 30 min to 1 hr for each taster, with no relation between level of expertise and the time it took to perform a task. Participants were instructed to taste and then to describe the wines using a set of terms developed by researchers in enology (Noble et al., 1987). This widely used terminology is known in the industry as the U. C. Davis Wine Wheel because its hierarchically organized terms are arrayed into three concentric circles. The Tier 1 terms are the most general and the Tier 3 terms are the most specific. *Fruit,* for example, a Tier 1 term, splits at Tier 2 into *citrus fruit, berry fruit, tree fruit, tropical fruit, dried fruit,* or *other fruit; tree fruit* itself splits at Tier 3 into *cherry, apricot, peach,* and *apple.* For each wine, participants checked off all terms that applied. They were also told that checking off a Tier 3 term implied that its corresponding Tier 1 and Tier 2 terms also applied.

This study was limited to an exploration of tasters' use of the Wine Wheel in the hope that it would make potential differences between experts and nonexperts more evident. Previous studies have found nonexperts to be particularly bad at describing aromas and flavors, but suggest that they may be as good as experts at judging sweetness (Lawless, 1984; Solomon, 1990).

Results

Number and specificity of features.   Analyses of the number and specificity of the features described support the claim of an increased differentiation associated with greater expertise. The more expert tasters described the wines using more and more specific features. The experts used an average of 5.0 flavor terms in each description, the intermediates used 3.1 terms, and the novices used 3.1 terms. An analysis of variance (ANOVA) of mean lengths of the descriptions was marginally significant, $F(2, 24) = 2.80$, $p = .08$, although the effect size was moderate ($\eta = .32$) and in the predicted direction. A planned linear contrast analysis, with weights set at 1, 0, and −1, more directly tested the prediction that experts would outperform the intermediates who would, in turn, outperform the novices and proved to be significant, $F(1, 24) = 4.43$, $p = .05$.

The specificity of the tasters' descriptions was assessed by calculating the percentage of each taster's terms that were chosen from each tier of the Wine Wheel. As can be seen in Table 1, the more expert tasters were more apt to describe the wines using more specific terms. On average, the experts chose 64% of their terms from the third, and most specific, tier, whereas the intermediates chose 46% of their terms, and the novices only 28% of their terms from that tier. A one-way ANOVA was conducted on the arcsin transformation of the percentage of each taster's terms that were from the third tier. The difference between groups was significant, $F(2, 25) = 4.06$, $p = .03$. As has been observed in other domains, wine experts would appear to identify more features and with greater specificity than do nonexperts.

TABLE 1
Mean Percentage of Terms That Were of Each Tier (From Least to
Most Specific) Chosen by Tasters in Experiment 1 at
Each Level of Expertise

Expertise Level	Specificity of Descriptions		
	Tier 1	Tier 2	Tier 3
Experts	17	20	64
Intermediates	31	24	46
Novices	25	38	28

Let us now look to whether the expert and nonexpert tasters, despite differences in the specificity of their descriptions, described wines in a manner suggesting a similar appreciation of an underlying organization of wines and wine features.

Organization implicit in descriptions.   Wine is as much a product of nature as a human artifact. It is possible that the tasters may have described the wines, whether intentionally or not, in a manner reflecting the natural division of grape type. If there is a difference between the experts and the novices in their conceptual organization of wines, it may be because the experts are able to appreciate this covariation but novices cannot. A superior expert ability to recognize the covariation of features by grape type may be due to the experts being able to recognize and describe wines with enough specificity to reflect this covariation. Novices may simply not be able to identify those features that covary. They may not be able to describe enough features specifically enough. Then again, it could be that novices do identify features that covary by grape type, but do not consider that covariation to be relevant to their judgments of types of wines. Therefore, we ask if the features described by tasters covaried with grape type and whether this covariation was reflected equally in the descriptions generated by the experts and nonexperts alike. Of course, it is also possible that neither the experts nor the nonexperts described the wines in ways that covaried significantly by grape type.

A regression analysis allows us a means of demonstrating the relation between tasters' descriptions and actual grape type. Each taster's descriptions were analyzed to see if the description of each wine was more highly correlated with descriptions of wines of the same grape than it was with descriptions of wines of different grapes. Each description was first represented as a pattern of ones and zeroes corresponding to whether or not a wine was judged to have a given feature. Recall that the features were arrayed in a hierarchical fashion on the Wine Wheel. The descriptions were therefore entered such that the selection of a more specific Tier 3 term, *lemon,* for example, necessarily implied the selection of its superordinate Tier 2 term, *citrus fruit,* as well as its Tier 1 term, *fruit.* (The tasters had been told explicitly of this implication.) This scoring resulted in a rough kind of weighting, such that if two wines were both described as having a Tier 3 feature, they effectively had three features in common; if two wines were both described as having a Tier 1 feature, they had only that one feature in common. The dependent variable of the regression analysis was the correlation coefficient of each pair of descriptions. The independent variable was a dummy coding of whether or not each pair of wines was of the same grape. To allow for comparison between groups, the correlation coefficient for each taster was transformed to a Fischer's z_r, thereby satisfying assumptions of normality (Howell, 1982).

The tasters did describe the wines in a manner that reflected a division by grape type. The mean expert z_r of .151 was significantly better than the zero correlation expected by chance, $t(7) = 3.13$, $p = .008$, as was the mean intermediate z_r of .142, $t(8) = 4.88$, $p < .001$, and the novice z_r of .159, $t(10) = 5.14$, $p < .001$. A one-way ANOVA showed that the groups did not differ significantly in the extent to which their assigning of features varied by grape.

Discussion

The covariation of features with classes provides indirect evidence of a coherent organization of the similarities and dissimilarities of the wines. Note, of course, that these results do not preclude there being other bases for organizing wines. Indeed, the regression indicates that grape type did not account for most of the variance between the wines. Bear in mind that these were very noisy data. Lehrer (1975, 1983) had not even found tasters able to convey information about wines at a level above chance, and Lawless (1984) and Solomon (1990) found nonexperts to be particularly bad at describing wine aromas. Furthermore, a researcher can select the wines in a stimulus set such that those of a particular grape type are very similar or very different (the wines in this study were selected to represent a range of similarity). That the regressions are significant at all is something of an achievement on the part of the tasters, given how complex wines are, how exceedingly difficult it is merely to describe them, and how variable are different bottles of the same wine (let alone different wines of the same grape).

What is striking about the results is that tasters received a structured set, whether structured artificially by an experimenter to covary by grape type or by natural forces, and they responded similarly to that structure. The covariation of features with grape type was no more represented in the expert than in the nonexpert descriptions.

One explanation for the lack of differences among the taster groups is that the effect of covariation of features in nature may be so compelling that it is manifested even in novice descriptions, without the tasters necessarily being explicitly aware of the covariations as such. We must be careful to distinguish between the wines' discontinuities in nature and the tasters' own classification judgments. It is not clear how experts and nonexperts would themselves weight the features in their Experiment 1 descriptions in determining classes; the tasters may not actually sort wines in a manner consistent with the simple covariation of features with grape type. For example, the gewürztraminer was frequently described by both experts and nonexperts as being *floral*. This feature may be heavily weighted by those tasters seeking to classify wines by grape type, for it is typically used to describe gewürztraminers, but it may not be weighted much at all by those tasters classifying the wines on the basis of how much they like them. The acquisition of expertise may entail a change in how features are weighted in determining classes. Experiment 2 is a more direct test of the tasters' classification judgments.

EXPERIMENT 2: SORTING TASK

The tasters' sense of the organization of wines that was implicit in the similarity of their Experiment 1 descriptions was made explicit in Experiment 2. Or more correctly, an organization was made explicit, for it was not clear that the two tasks would yield the same results. The tasters were instructed to sort the wines such that the more similar wines were to be placed into the same groups. A comparison of the results of Experiments 1 and 2 allows us to explore whether the experts' and nonexperts' judgments were embedded in the same conceptual framework and whether those judgments equally reflected the structure implied by the covariation of features in their Experiment 1 descriptions. It was not even clear at the outset that all tasters could summon a coherent system on which to base their judgments.

In this experiment, the tasters considered the entire array of 10 wines at once and were thereby led indirectly to base their similarity judgments on features or dimensions pertaining to a number, if not all, of the wines, rather than make their judgments in an exhaustive series of pair by pair comparisons. Lawless (1989) found that participants instructed to sort an array of odors directly into groups produced highly interpretable results. The tasters in the present study also found the task quite natural. Indeed, many of the tasters at all three levels of expertise, when faced with the array of wines, began to sort and classify the wines even before they had been instructed to do so.

Procedure

Participants were provided with the same 10 wines they had described in Experiment 1 (see Appendix C), although they were not told that these were the same wines they had previously tasted. They were asked to sort the wines into four groups such that the wines in the same group were more similar to each other than they were to wines in other groups (some participants then sorted the wines into subgroups as well). The participants were also asked to provide the reasons for their sortings.

Results

The results of the sorting task demonstrated that experts categorize wines differently than do intermediates and novices. The difference between the experts' and the nonexperts' judgments about which wines belonged in the same class was significant, $Q(1) = 3.87, p = .05$, as assessed by Cochran's test, a nonparametric measure akin to the chi-square and recommended by Fleiss (1981) for making group comparisons of categorical data using repeated measures.

The experts' explicit justifications of their sortings indicate that they did indeed base their classification judgments on supposed grape type. Six of the eight experts used grape type or a combination of grape and region to justify their classifications (although not always correctly); only two gave single feature rationales for their sortings (e.g., fruity). Most tellingly, in contrast to the experts, no intermediates or novices mentioned grape type or wine-making region in explaining their judgments. This is in stark contrast to the Experiment 1 finding that for experts and nonexperts alike, descriptions covaried by grape type. To be sure, the nonexperts based their classification judgments on perceptual features, but they used single, nonorthogonal features or dimensions (e.g., fruity, bitter, sweet, good, complex).

Covariation of Features With Classes

One of the functions of categories is to support the induction of features. Consider whether experts and nonexperts differed in the extent to which their Experiment 2 classification judgments corresponded to covariations of the features they described in Experiment 1. The wine descriptions produced in Experiment 1 were again analyzed by regression to determine if wines of the same class were described more similarly than were wines of different classes. However, rather than define classes by actual grape type, they were defined according to each taster's Experiment 2 sortings. As before, the derived correlations were converted to Fischer z_rs to allow for comparisons between groups.

The tasters' wine descriptions were more similar within class than between classes. That is, descriptions of features covaried by supposed class membership more than would be expected by chance for the intermediates, $t(8) = 5.00, p < .001$, and novices, $t(10) = 3.91, p = .002$, as well as for the experts, $t(7) = 3.84, p = .003$. The mean expert z_r of .348 was significantly better than the intermediate z_r of .071 and novice z_r of .062, as indicated by both an ANOVA, $F(2, 25) = 11.30, p < .001$, and linear contrast, $F(1, 25) = 18.89, p < .001$.

The superior expert classification of wines is most striking when viewed in conjunction with the regression analyses of Experiment 1. The expert descriptions covaried significantly better by their sorted categories than they did by actual grape type, $t(7) = 3.15$, $p = .008$, whereas the correlations of descriptions by categories were significantly worse for the intermediate, $t(8) = 2.33$, $p = .05$, and novice, $t(10) = 2.58$, $p = .03$, tasters when compared to their Experiment 1 groupings by actual grape type.

Discussion

The experts and nonexperts differed in how they understood their perceptions to relate to their organizing of the wine world. Most experts explicitly based their classification judgments on grape type, a qualitatively different system of organization than that used by the nonexperts. Even the experts' "errors" underscore the extent to which they based their classification judgments on assessments of grape type. For example, those experts who sorted the pinot gris with the chardonnays actually identified the wine, incorrectly, as a chardonnay. It is even possible that experts' explicit knowledge of the features that are common to wines of a given grape type may have contributed to the similarities in the descriptions of wines of the same type. If tasters presumed a wine to be of a particular grape they may have been more likely to judge it to have a feature they know to be typical of that type. For example, believing a wine to be a sauvignon blanc, tasters may change their thresholds for just how "grassy" the wine would have to be to call it grassy.

It is not surprising that experts should categorize on the basis of grape type, for it is part of their specialized functioning in the field. They are commonly called on to identify the grapes that make up a wine; many even study grape type as a causal factor underlying a wine's observable features. This greater conceptual knowledge would appear to be associated with a difference between experts and nonexperts in how they assigned importance to observed features in determining class membership.

The novices and intermediates did not intentionally classify the wines by grape type, despite the fact that they described wines of the same grape type significantly more similarly than they did wines of different types. Rather, nonexperts claimed to classify on only one or two salient features. Granted, the wines sorted together by nonexperts were described significantly more similarly than were those sorted apart, but the level of association was worse than it was when they were sorted by actual grape type. The significance of the nonexpert classification-by-description regression could be due to the fact that choosing one feature to define a cluster necessarily entails the covariation of other features because the features themselves may not be independent in nature. The key here is that the novices and intermediates neither showed explicit awareness of regular variation by grape type nor took advantage of it in making classification judgments, whereas the experts did. There would appear to be a reweighting, a restructuring, of the system in which classification judgments are embedded.

GENERAL DISCUSSION

Whether driven by conscious deliberation or by the predispositions of a perceptual system, class membership is not a relation that necessarily exists independent of the observer. The fact that wine categories are based, at least in part, on perceived features and that these features are combined in nonarbitrary ways is not in doubt. In Experiment 1, tasters at all levels of expertise described wines of the same grape more similarly than they did wines of different grapes. They identified features in accord with a natural division of the biological world. However, in Experiment 2 the novices, unlike the experts, did not consider grape type to be a basis for classification judgments despite the fact that their descriptions of the wines covaried by grape type significantly better than they did by the classes that they actually created. Having described a set of objects with an underlying category structure did not guarantee that novices' similarity judgments would preserve those classes. The results suggest that the acquisition of wine expertise entails a change in tasters' systems of classification, a change in the basis by which similarity is assessed.

The acquisition of wine expertise may entail a movement from a more perceptually to a more conceptually driven recognition of feature salience. Of course, distinguishing the perceptual from the conceptual has proven to be among the knottiest of philosophical problems. The change in tasters' classification judgments could be characterized as reflecting either conceptual change or perceptual change, depending on where the line between them is drawn. Consider the distinction at one extreme. If we assumed a modular cognitive architecture of the sort described (although in varying ways) by Fodor (1983) and Marr (1982), we could restrict the perceptual to that level of processing whose output only can be affected by conscious thought. Leslie (1988) discussed the Pulfrich double pendulum illusion as an example of a perceptual representation impervious to the influence of beliefs: Despite your knowledge of the laws of physics, you cannot help but see one object pass through another. By this definition, to the extent that the assigning of feature saliencies was part of the conscious act of classification, it would be a conceptual process.

The point of raising the distinction between the conceptual and the perceptual is not to take a definitive stand on the difference between the two; there are a host of rejoinders to the previous argument. The point, rather, is that it allows us to focus on characterizing the processes that distinguish experts from novices. The intuitive appeal of the perceptual–conceptual distinction is that experts and novices appear to agree on what it is to constitute an attribute of a wine, on the perceived features as it were, but they disagree over how such attributes are to be weighted for classification. Moreover, the experts' system of classification is associated with their having explicit causal explanations, a conceptual basis, for why the wines have the features they do.

The experts in this article classified wines in a manner more consistent with a covariation of features, perhaps because they, and not the novices, could supply a causal explanation—grape type—that would motivate that covariation. In debriefing, experts said that the grape type caused the wines to have many of the features they did. Indeed, in the wine literature a wine's *aroma* refers, strictly speaking, only to those odors caused by the grape (*bouquet* refers to those odors caused by the wine-making process, such as from the effects of putting the grape pressings into oaken barrels). The experts may have better captured the range of their descriptions in their classifications because they had a causal model of wine that supported the induction of such features. By contrast, in the absence of a theoretically driven basis for classification, of a coherent conceptual system in which to ground their judgments of similarity, the novice and intermediate wine tasters evidently resorted to local strategies based on single features. This finding has a precedent in the categorization literature.

Medin, Wattenmaker, and Hampson (1987) had participants sort a set of stimuli. The features of the stimuli (e.g., the numbers of appendages and colors of fictitious animals or the various symptoms of diseases) were designed with an underlying structure, such that categorization based on the covariation of features would yield better classes than would categorization by single defining features. That is, exemplars of the same category would share more features with each other than they would with exemplars of other categories. Surprisingly, most participants used the less optimal strategy of sorting by single dimensions or strings of dimensions, rather than on the basis of a covariation of features. It was only when the experimenters provided some thematic or conceptual justifications for why the symptoms cooccurred in given patterns that the participants made categorization judgments in accordance with the covariation of such features. It would seem that the wine experts in these studies were more able to conjure such conceptual justifications than were the nonexperts.

As Berlin (1978), Brown (1958), and Rosch et al. (1976) suggested, differences in classification schemes are likely tied to differences between groups in the nature of their functioning in the domain. Experts, in the course of being experts, require a framework that organizes and explains the important features in their domains. They are often called on to name and describe wines and to make featural inferences about other wines of the same type.

The novices and experts may have considered their judgments as relevant to different ranges of objects. Experts appeared to consider the array of 10 wines in the context of the range of wine classes. Novices may not even have wine categories as such. Keil (1989) posited that, in the absence of a theoretically driven understanding of classification, people will resort to perceptual similarity as a default basis for classification. A default sense of similarity implies that there be a default sense of what is to count as a feature, a default sense of how such features are to be weighted in classification judgments, and, by extension, a default set of classes. Surely, if we do have a default sense of gustatory or olfactory similarity, it is more appropriate to making gross distinctions among the classes of potable and nonpotable or sweet and nonsweet fluids than among types of wines. Retailers anecdotally report that novice wine customers usually request a wine in terms of a single highly salient feature (e.g., sweetness or bitterness). Indeed, in this study, the kinds of justifications novices gave for their classifications were not specific to wine categories, but could just as easily be used to differentiate more general food or drink categories. Novices may roughly be able to identify the same features in wines that experts do, and these features may well covary by grape type, but it would not be cognitively economical for novices to devote much attention to those features if they supported a differentiation of classes of little importance to them.

Occupying the gray area between the conceptual and the perceptual, wine tasting is a domain of particular interest because both the experts' and the novices' systems of classification captured perceived features, but they were not equally determined by them. We would expect to find a similar reweighting of features in the acquisition of expertise in other domains in which there is general agreement as to what is to count as a feature but in which experts are required to make qualitatively different use of the classes they create. For example, in music, novices may have strong perceptual predispositions driving an initial recognition of saliences and similarity, but conceptual understanding may lead experts to a different crafting of meaning out of the senses (e.g., Krumhansl, 1979). Although Berlin (1978) and others have shown that certain distinctions in the biological world "cry out to be named" (p. 11), because of perceptual dissimilarities, there is great debate about the role of causal explanations in children's and adults' inferences about features and classes of entities (Atran, 1994; Solomon, Johnson, Zaitchik, & Carey, 1996). Of course, there are also many domains in which experts' and novices' systems of classification are similar. The acquisition of expertise in these domains may be marked by increasing perceptual differentiation, but no qualitative change in feature weighting need be posited. Experts may classify at a subordinate level in a hierarchy of classes but in a manner that preserved the general order.

Wine tasting would appear to be a domain in which differences between experts and novices in how they create classes of wines is associated with qualitative differences in their attributions of a causal basis to classes of wines and their features. These studies do not address how it is that experts come to grape type as a causal explanatory concept; that would take a longitudinal study. What these studies do suggest is that wine expertise, however it is acquired, involves a conceptual change, in Kitcher's (1988) sense. For the experts, and not the novices, grape type was a fundamental explanatory concept: It explained regularities reflected in their descriptions and motivated their organizing the world based on those regularities. In short, experts would appear to be expert because of the order they perceive in nature, but also because of that they bring to it.

ACKNOWLEDGMENTS

For their intellectual, oenological, and humanitarian aid, I toast David Alcott, Rebecca Alssid, Henry Barbour, Liz Bishop, Linda Tickle Degnen, Fred Ek, Harvey Finkel, Bill Gerin, Kelly Jaakkola, Harry Lawless, Danica Mijovic, Steve Mosher, Bill Nesto, Ann Noble, Michael O'Mahony, Richard Sanford, Virginia Slaughter, Beate Sodian, Cristina Sorrentino, Josh Tenenbaum, Steffen Werner, the Boston University Certificate Program in the Culinary Arts, the editors, and anonymous reviewers. I especially thank Roger Brown, Susan Carey, and Drazen Prelec, without whose support this work would have rotted on the vine. Cheers.

REFERENCES

Amerine, M. A., & Roessler, E. B. (1983). *Wines: Their sensory evaluation.* New York: Freeman.

Atran, S. (1994). Core domains versus scientific theories: Evidence from systematics and Itzaj-Maya folkbiology. In L. Hirschfeld & S. A. Gelman (Eds.), *Mapping the mind: Domain-specificity in cognition and culture* (pp. 316–340). New York: Cambridge University Press.

Berlin, B. (1978). Ethnobiological classification. In E. Rosch & B. B. Lloyd (Eds.), *Cognition and categorization* (pp. 9–26). Hillsdale, NJ: Lawrence Erlbaum Associates, Inc.

Berlin, B. (1981). Speculation on the growth of ethnobiological nomenclature. *Language in Society, 1,* 51–86.

Biederman, I., & Shiffrar, M. M. (1987). Sexing day-old chicks: A case study and expert systems analysis of a difficult perceptual-learning task. *Journal of Experimental Psychology: Learning, Memory, and Cognition, 13,* 640–645.

Brown, R. W. (1958). How shall a thing be called? *Psychological Review, 65,* 14–21.

Carey, S. (1988). Conceptual differences between adults and children. *Mind and Language, 3,* 167–181.

Carey, S. (1991). Knowledge acquisition: Enrichment or conceptual change? In S. Carey & R. Gelman (Eds.), *The epigenesis of mind: Essays on biology and cognition* (pp. 257–292). Hillsdale, NJ: Lawrence Erlbaum Associates, Inc.

Chase, W. G., & Simon, H. A. (1973). Perception in chess. *Cognitive Psychology, 4,* 55–81.

Chastrette, M., Elmouaffek, A., & Sauvegrain, P. (1988). A multidimensional statistical study of similarities between 74 notes used in perfumery. *Chemical Senses, 13,* 295–305.

Chi, M. T. H., Feltovich, P. J., & Glaser, R. (1981). Categorization and representation of physics problems by experts and novices. *Cognitive Science, 5,* 121–152.

Chi, M. T. H., Hutchinson, J. E., & Robin, A. F. (1989). How inferences about normal domain-related concepts can be constrained by structured knowledge. *Merrill-Palmer Quarterly, 35,* 27–62.

Chi, M. T. H., & Koeske, R. (1983). Network representation of a child's dinosaur knowledge. *Developmental Psychology, 19,* 29–39.

de Groot, A. (1965). *Thought and choice in chess.* The Hague, The Netherlands: Mouton.

Dougherty, J. W. D. (1978). Salience and relativity in classification. *American Ethnologist, 5,* 66–80.

Fleiss, J. A. (1981). *Statistical methods for rates and proportions.* New York: Wiley.

Fodor, J. (1983). *The modularity of mind.* Cambridge, MA: MIT Press.

Gallistel, C. R., Brown, A. L., Carey, S., Gelman, R., & Keil, F. C. (1991). In S. Carey & R. Gelman (Eds.), *The epigenesis of mind: Essays on biology and cognition* (pp. 3–36). Hillsdale, NJ: Lawrence Erlbaum Associates, Inc.

Gibson, J. J. (1966). *The senses considered as perceptual systems*. Boston: Houghton Mifflin.

Gibson, J. J., & Gibson, E. J. (1955). Perceptual learning: Differentiation or enrichment. *Psychological Review, 62,* 32–41.

Gobbo, C., & Chi, M. T. H. (1986). How knowledge is structured and used by expert and novice children. *Cognitive Development, 1,* 221–237.

Howell, D. C. (1982). *Statistical methods for psychology*. Boston: Duxbury.

Keil, F. C. (1989). *Concepts, kinds, and cognitive development*. Cambridge, England: Cambridge University Press.

Kitcher, P. (1988). The child as parent of the scientist. *Mind and Language, 3,* 217–228.

Krumhansl, C. L. (1979). The psychological representation of musical pitch in a tonal context. *Cognitive Psychology, 11,* 346–374.

Kuhn, T. S. (1970). *The structure of scientific revolutions* (2nd ed.). Chicago: University of Chicago Press.

Kuhn, T. S. (1977). *The essential tension*. Chicago: University of Chicago Press.

Kuhn, T. S. (1983). Commensurability, comparability, and communicability. In P. Asquith & T. Nickles (Eds.), *PSA 1982* (pp. 669–688). East Lansing, MI: Philosophy of Science Association.

Lakoff, G. (1986). *Women, fire, and dangerous things: What categories tell about the nature of thought*. Chicago: University of Chicago Press.

Lawless, H. T. (1984). Flavor description of white wine by expert and nonexpert wine consumers. *Journal of Food Science, 49,* 120–123.

Lawless, H. T. (1988). Odour description and odour classification revisited. In D. M. M. Thomson (Ed.), *Food and acceptability* (pp. 27–40). London: Elsevier.

Lawless, H. T. (1989). Exploration of fragrance categories and ambiguous odors using multidimensional scaling and cluster analysis. *Chemical Senses, 14,* 349–360.

Lehrer, A. (1975). Talking about wine. *Language, 51,* 901–923.

Lehrer, A. (1983). *Wine and conversation*. Bloomington: Indiana University Press.

Leslie, A. M. (1988). The necessity of illusion: Perception and thought in infancy. In L. Weiskrantz (Ed.), *Thought without language* (pp. 185–210). Oxford, England: Oxford Science Publications.

Lunn, J. H. (1948). Chick sexing. *American Scientist, 36,* 280–287.

Malt, B. C., & Smith, E. E. (1984). Correlated properties in natural categories. *Journal of Verbal Learning and Verbal Behavior, 23,* 250–269.

Marr, D. (1982). *Vision*. San Francisco: Freeman.

Medin, D. L., Wattenmaker, W. D., & Hampson, S. E. (1987). Family resemblance, conceptual cohesiveness, and category construction. *Cognitive Psychology, 19,* 242–279.

Nersessian, N. J. (1992). How do scientists think? Capturing the dynamics of conceptual change in science. In R. N. Giere (Ed.), *Cognitive models of science: Minnesota studies in the philosophy of science* (Vol. 15, pp. 3–44). Minneapolis: University of Minnesota Press.

Noble, A. C., Arnold, R. A., Buechsenstein, J., Leach, E. J., Schmidt, J. O., & Stern, P. M. (1987). Modification of a standardized system of wine aroma terminology. *American Journal of Enology and Viticulture, 38,* 143–146.

Robinson, J. (1986). *Vines, grapes, and wines*. New York: Knopf.

Rosch, E., & Mervis, C. B. (1975). Family resemblance: Studies in the internal structure of categories. *Cognitive Psychology, 7,* 573–605.

Rosch, E., Mervis, C. B., Gray, W. D., Johnson, D. M., & Boyes-Braem, P. (1976). Basic objects in natural categories. *Cognitive Psychology, 8,* 382–439.

Solomon, G. E. A. (1990). The psychology of novice and expert wine talk. *American Journal of Psychology, 103,* 495–517.

Solomon, G. E. A., Johnson, S. C., Zaitchik, D., & Carey, S. (1996). Like father, like son: Young children's understanding of biological inheritance. *Child Development, 67,* 151–171.

Tanaka, J. W., & Taylor, M. (1991). Object categories and expertise: Is the basic level in the eye of the beholder? *Cognitive Psychology, 23,* 457–482.

APPENDIX A
Novice Questionnaire

Participants who answered "yes" to more than one of the following were not considered to be novices:

1. Have you ever taken a wine-tasting course?
2. Have you ever bought a bottle of wine for yourself (other than a celebratory bottle of champagne) that cost more than $15?
3. Was wine generally served with dinner as you grew up?
4. Were your parents, a spouse, or roommate particularly knowledgeable about wine?
5. Do you generally order wine from a wine list in restaurants?

APPENDIX B
Wines Used in Triangle Test

Wine	Year	Region	Cost
Chateau Plessis	1989	Entre-deux-mers, Bordeaux, France	$5.99
Chateau Lalande	1989	Entre-deux-mers, Bordeaux, France	$5.99
Chateau Recougne	1988	Graves, Bordeaux, France	$5.99
Chateau Claron	1988	Graves, Bordeaux, France	$6.49

APPENDIX C
Wines Used in Experiments 1 and 2, by Grape

Wine	Year	Region	Cost
Chardonnay			
Rothbury Estate	1989	Hunter Valley, Australia	$10.99
Sanford Winery	1988	Santa Barbara, California	$14.99
Johnson Turnbull	1988	Napa Valley, California	$12.99
Whitehall Lane (Le Petit)	1989	Napa Valley, California	$ 8.99
William Fèvre	1988	Chablis, France	$13.49
Sauvignon blanc			
Murphy-Goode, Fumé blanc	1988	Alexander Valley, California	$ 8.99
Clos de la Crele	1988	Sancerre, France	$12.99
Pinot gris (Pinot grigio)			
Furlan	1988	Friuli, Italy	$10.99
Trimbach	1988	Alsace, France	$ 9.99
Gewürztraminer			
Trimbach	1988	Alsace, France	$ 9.99

THE JOURNAL OF THE LEARNING SCIENCES, 6(1), 61–89

The Role of Extreme Case Reasoning in Instruction for Conceptual Change

Aletta Zietsman

Department of Physics
University of the Witwatersrand, South Africa

John Clement

Scientific Reasoning Research Institute
University of Massachusetts at Amherst

Although it is common to see extreme case reasoning included in lists of expert heuristics for problem solving, little work has been reported on the role that extreme cases can play in learning that leads to conceptual change. Evidence is presented from video tapes of think-aloud tutoring sessions to document the learning from extreme cases in a unit about levers for seventh graders. The observations support the view that one role of extreme cases is to provide a firm data point or comparison that helps students to establish an ordinal relation between two given variables. Two new additional roles for extreme cases in fostering learning are also identified: (a) their role in *activating an intuition,* often in the form of a *perceptual motor schema,* that is used in *constructing an imageable, intuitively, grounded, explanatory model* as opposed to an empirical rule; and (b) their role in *facilitating the formation of new causal variables.* Pending confirmation of similar effects in other subject areas, these roles are candidates for being included in a set of general learning strategies for science instruction. This illustrates the function that "learning-aloud" studies can play in documenting new types of learning processes and instructional strategies. The study highlights the importance for instructional design of research that uncovers students' existing knowledge structures and natural reasoning processes. The study suggests that explanatory model construction, causal relation construction, and concept formation can result from such instructional designs. The extent to which these three outcomes are evidence for strong conceptual change is also discussed.

Requests for reprints should be sent to John Clement, Scientific Reasoning Research Institute, Hasbrouck Laboratory, University of Massachusetts, Amherst, MA 01003. E-mail: clement@srri.umass.edu

The use of extreme cases as a reasoning strategy by experts has been documented in historical studies (Nersessian, 1992) and expert thinking-aloud studies (Clement, 1989, 1991). The use of extreme case reasoning as an instructional strategy is not as well documented (for an exception, see Zietsman & Hewson's, 1986, description of computer-based instruction that uses extreme cases in dissonance generating situations). This article examines the ways in which extreme case reasoning facilitated learning in a study of students' learning about levers. The purpose of this article is to use qualitative analyses of tutoring transcripts as an empirical base to develop grounded hypotheses for thinking about the roles extreme cases can play in learning and teaching.

The context of this study is a broader program of research and development in which the major goals are to:

1. Identify students' persistent misconceptions, or alternative conceptions as we prefer to call them, that conflict with currently accepted theory.
2. Identify students' positive preconceptions, or anchoring ideas as we call them, that are largely in agreement with the scientist's ideas.
3. Build on the students' positive preconceptions in designing experimental lessons that deal with their alternative conceptions.
4. Use tapes of tutoring trials with the lessons to criticize and improve them.
5. Analyze the processes occurring in successful lessons to develop more general models of learning and teaching principles.

This article is structured as follows. We first review descriptions from prior research of different mechanisms by which extreme cases may contribute to thinking. We next give an overview of the design of the tutoring study and then present protocol evidence to illustrate students' learning. Finally, in our discussions of student learning, we concentrate on the following two issues: (a) asking *whether* the extreme cases in an experimental lesson on levers facilitated learning and (b) constructing hypotheses grounded in case study data that explain *how* the extreme cases facilitated learning.

PREVIOUS RESEARCH ON EXTREME
CASE REASONING

Although it is common to mention extreme cases as an expert heuristic in problem solving (Polya, 1954), little work has been reported on the roles that extreme case examples may play in learning. The traditional view of the way in which extreme cases contribute to thinking is as a *check* on a problem solution as follows.

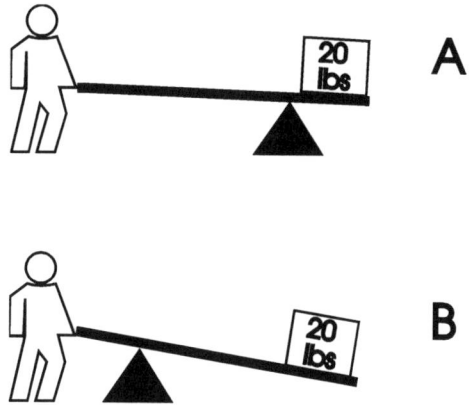

FIGURE 1   Extreme cases providing data points.

A Check on a Problem Solution

When the answer to a problem is expressed as a mathematical function, the correctness of the function can be checked conveniently by plugging in extreme values, such as zero or infinity, for the independent variable (Polya, 1954). Often, one can infer from the physical situation (independently from the mathematics) what the answer should be in this case and see whether the function gives the same prediction.

Generating a "Direction of Change" Functional Relation

A less commonly recognized, but important role in science is to use the extreme case to help generate a less quantitative, direction of change relation or ordinal function of the form "when X increases, Y increases (or decreases)." Such a relation can be inferred from the knowledge of two data points, $(X0, Y0)$ and $(X1, Y1)$, and the assumption of a monotonic relation between the variables (that Y always moves in the same direction as X increases). The comparison of the two lever situations in Figure 1 illustrates this point. In general, students know intuitively that it will be very easy to lift the load in Case A and very hard in Case B; hence, one may infer that, as the distance from the load to the fulcrum decreases, the force needed to lift the load would also decrease.

The extreme case can provide one of the "data points" needed to infer the more general direction of change relation. This role should be useful for learning basic ideas in science, in which such relations are ubiquitous. It can be argued that such relations also provide an intuitive underpinning for the understanding of mathematical relations in science. Weld (1990) developed an artificial intelligence (AI) program that explores some of the issues involved in implementing similar types of extreme case reasoning.

Galileo's (1638/1954) famous extreme case of an object rolling on a plane of zero inclination also provides an intuitive starting point from which to develop and better understand a generalized, mathematical theory of motion. He reasoned that because a ball rolling on a plane that slopes down to the right will accelerate, a ball rolling on a plane that rises to the right will decelerate, and a ball rolling on a plane that is horizontal (parallel to the surface of the Earth) will neither accelerate nor decelerate.

Other Roles of Extreme Cases in Learning

Nersessian (1989, 1992) reviewed some other extreme cases used by Galileo and hypothesized that most thought experiments (of which, according to Nersessian, extreme cases are one type) work via a process of mental simulation. The mental simulation required is linked to perceptual processing and contrasted with propositional processing (Nersessian, 1992). In this article, we provide some support for viewing extreme cases as involving perceptual motor schemas, as opposed to merely invoking verbal rules (e.g., "more A means more B"). This provides some initial empirical evidence that is very compatible with Nersessian's view.

In this article, we also provide evidence for two other roles of extreme cases that appear to be important learning strategies but to our knowledge have not been discussed in the literature. These are the functions of (a) aiding in the construction of a qualitative, explanatory model for a system and (b) fostering the isolation of new causal variables in a system. We expose these roles via excerpts from thinking-aloud tutoring studies with seventh graders learning about the behavior of levers.

CHILDREN LEARNING CONCEPTIONS ABOUT LEVERS

An example of a generic levers question is given in Figure 2. (The labels for variables have been added to the figure and were not seen by the students.)

Students were told that the boards are considered to be light, but strong and inflexible (so as not to affect the outcome) and are hinged to the fulcrums. We refer frequently to the lever arms (dLF and dEF), as well as the load and the effort. The children were asked to refer to the fulcrum as the turning point, a term that was thought to be more descriptive and perhaps more suggestive for them. In pre- and posttest interviews and lesson interviews, we asked questions about such drawings of "generic" levers. In transfer questions in both the lesson and posttest, real levers, such as nail clippers, were also presented for discussion.

FIGURE 2   Example of a generic
levers question:
  Question: Where would it be easier
  to keep the board with the 20-lb
  load on it level?
  (a) In case A.
  (b) In case B.
  (c) The same force would be
       needed in case A and case B.
  Confidence Scale:
  (a) Just a blind guess.
  (b) Not very confident.
  (c) Fairly confident.
  (d) I'm sure I'm right.

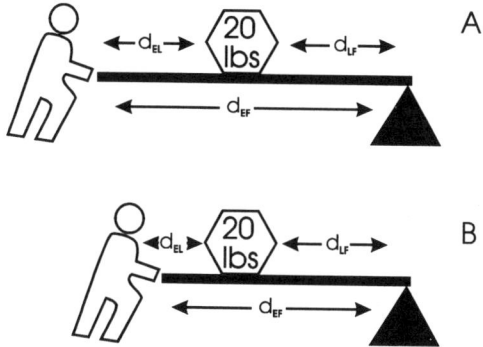

    The data reported in this article comes from a set of studies reported in Zietsman (1991). The set comprised a sequence of lesson design and evaluation activities including diagnostic studies ($n = 242$), exploratory tutoring ($n = 37$), and two systematic tutoring studies ($n = 6 \times 2$). Before and after the systematic tutoring sessions, clinical interviews were conducted on pre- and posttests with the all the participants. During the tutoring sessions, students were asked to think aloud as much as possible. Detailed analyses of transcripts from the first systematic tutoring group, focusing on why learning processes did or did not occur, were used to criticize and modify the instruction for the second group of students in tutoring interviews. The focus in this article is on an analysis of protocol data from this last cycle of tutoring interviews (called the experimental group) and specifically from sections dealing with Class II levers (those in which the load is between the fulcrum and the effort). We use this data to formulate grounded hypotheses about whether learning occurred and why.

Exploratory Work: Students' Preconceptions About Levers

Alternative conceptions about levers.   Seventh-grade students from three schools in Western Massachusetts were interviewed in the first, more exploratory cycle of the study. The first set of interviews was aimed at identifying the students' preconceptions concerning levers. The term preconception is used to refer to the conceptions students appeared to have just before the study. In the diagnostic question comparing Class II levers shown in Figure 3, the only change in variable, from the expert's point of view, is the effort arm (dEF). One can conclude that, because

$$\text{Effort} \times \text{dEF} = \text{Load} \times \text{dLF},$$

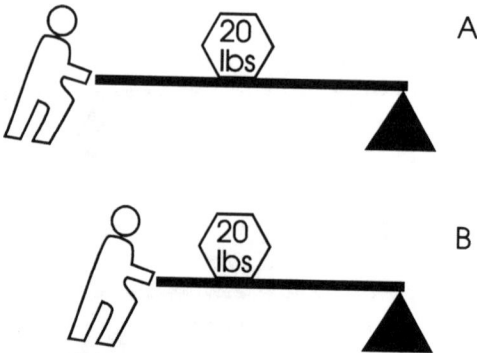

FIGURE 3   Comparing Class II levers: Target question.
Question: Where would it be easier to keep the board with the 20-lb load on it level?
(a) In Case A.
(b) In Case B.
(c) The same force would be needed in Case A and Case B.

the effort required to balance the load in Case B would be greater than that required in Case A.

However, many students exhibited one of two alternative conceptions (misconceptions) in their explanations for this pretest question. The first, held by the majority of students, is illustrated by EE5's explanation that a smaller load-effort (dEL) separation in Situation B resulted in less effort (I = interviewer; gaps in transcript line numbers indicate places where sections of the transcript were not included to save space):

3   EE5:   Well, in B I think. [less effort]
5   EE5:   its harder ... to control it and stuff [in A]

This "control" idea conflicts with accepted physical theory in this context. Using this "control conception," children appear to think that the closer one's hand is to the load, the easier it is to control—which is true in many everyday situations.

The second alternative conception, observed for the same question, also relates the load-effort separation and the effort (i.e., an increase in dEL) results in a decreased effort:

13   EE2:   [It is easier in Case A], because the weight of the 20 lb is more spread out and farther away.
14   I: Farther away?
15   EE2:   Farther away from where you would be holding it up and the other 20 lb would be right near you in Case B, and so it'd be harder to hold up.

Students using this conception in Class II lever situations would answer correctly. However, this nongeneralizable or limited conception can only be applied successfully to Class II levers. It gives an incorrect prediction, for example, when applied to the problem in Figure 1. One can therefore not consider this a good intuitive conception from which to develop a principle of levers that is compatible to the physicist's, who tend never to refer to the distance between the effort and the load at all.

Examples of Positive Preconceptions: Spontaneous, Student-Generated Ideas That We Incorporated Into the Instructional Strategy

A number of students' spontaneous ideas emerged during the exploratory tutoring phase of the research that were eventually used in the final systematic tutoring sequence. We give two examples. The first is the idea that the "fulcrum can help" support the load and comes from Meaghan, when she discussed a problem similar to the problem in Figure 3, except that the triangular fulcrum was replaced by a table, and the boards were of equal length, with the weight closer to the table in B. (M is Meaghan and I is the interviewer.)

1	M:	I think once again it'd be easier in Case B, because
2		when the weight is farther away from the table
3		itself then it puts more stress on the board [pause]
		And [pause]
5		Oh wait. Actually, I think it'd be easier in A,
6		because you're closer to the weight and, like I said
		before with the seesaw, things like that would be
		easier [pause].
9		Uhm ... I'm not sure.
10	I:	What is puzzling you now?
11	M:	It seems that in B it'd be easier because it's
		closer to the table, so the table is holding more
		weight than you are
13		But in A if it would be so, it would change what I
		said for all the other's answers—all the other's.

In line 1, Meaghan gives a response that she marked "I'm sure I'm right" on the confidence scale while she was starting to talk. In line 5, she realizes that this answer is different from her others (five other lever situations, such as see-saws) and this apparently caused dissonance (lines 13–14). In the other answers, she consistently used the "load closer to the effort, easier for the person" misconception (the control conception). In line 11, the idea of "a fulcrum helping," inferred from Meaghan's statement that "it's closer to the table, so the table holds more weight than you are," was recognized for the first time in the study. We in fact eventually built this idea into our instructional sequence. This reinforces our view that hidden natural

TABLE 1
Abbreviations and Coding for Patterns of Speech

Abbreviation	Patterns of Speech	Coding
c_c	You just have more control over it	control conception
	Its harder to control [weight farther]	
	[Easier closer] because the weight is right there	
share model	[They are] sharing the weight evenly	share model
	[They hold the same] its spread evenly	
f-h model	The thing holds the other 10 lb up	fulcrum-helps model
	This [fulcrum] is there pushing up	
c_{po}	The man has to hold 20 lb, because there is	powerless-object
	just this [fulcrum] supporting it	conception
	The other 10 lb is just resting on this [fulcrum]	
c_l	[Easier] because the weight is ... farther away	limited/nongeneralizable
	from where you would be holding it	conception

knowledge structures can be found and tapped in research driven curriculum development. A summary of conceptions found and typical patterns of speech used to identify them appears in Table 1.

In an even more striking example of a positive naive reasoning process, Brian (also in the exploratory interviews) spontaneously extended the Figure 2a situation into an extreme case. In this excerpt, Brian is thinking about a summary of "what makes it easier to hold the load." (B is Brian and I is the interviewer.)

54 B: Uhm ... what makes it easier? I think it makes
          it easier if—can I put this on the triangle?
          [makes drawing]
56   I think its easier when the load is on that end
          of the board, right near the block because
58 I: OK, let's call that the turning point
59 B: Yeah, near the turning point because then the
          force of the load, I mean is supported.
61 I: OK so you said one thing: the load is, if the
          load is near to the turning point—maybe you
          can write that down, that's one thing.
64   Load near to the turning point. [and writes]
65 I: And do you think, ah—is there anything else
          that matters?
67 B: Uh how long the board is. Because if you have
          like, because if you're holding that same board
          with the force there, and the same force was

71

right on top of there [indicates load], then
it'd be easier [in the first case]—or you were holding it
when the board went all the way to the other
end of the library you'd barely have to hold it
at all.

Brian, as opposed to Meaghan, gave the correct answers throughout his interview but supported by the nongeneralizable conception (i.e., the further the load is from the person, the easier). In the transcript excerpt presented, he differentiates for the first time the load-fulcrum distance as important, reasoning that the load is supported by the turning point (lines 59–60). His imaginary extension of the lever arm to "the other end of the library" (the interview occurred in the library) is a first-class, playful example of an extreme case and is obviously meaningful to him: "You'd barely have to hold it at all." This is one of the early findings that encouraged us to build extreme cases into our instruction. This reinforced our view that hidden natural reasoning processes can be found and tapped in research driven curriculum development.

DESCRIPTION OF LEVERS LESSON

The Class II levers lessons attempted to ground instruction in the students' naive ideas like those previously mentioned that were in agreement with scientific theory. Two teaching techniques employing this grounding principle were used in the lesson: (a) an analogy-based bridging approach (Clement, 1988, 1993) and (b) an extended sequence on reasoning from extreme cases.

Analogical Bridging Sequence

Target question.   The diagnostic question in Figure 3 was also used as a target situation in the lesson. The function of the target question was to identify a student's initial and final knowledge state and to give the lesson developers a concrete subgoal in attaining student understanding.

Anchoring example.   A much easier case (analogous to the target example) followed the target question and was viewed as an anchoring example. In the anchoring example for the Class II levers lesson, two people are sharing a 20-lb load (see Figure 4). Evidence for the existence of an anchoring example, defined theoretically as an example activating an intuitive knowledge structure in rough

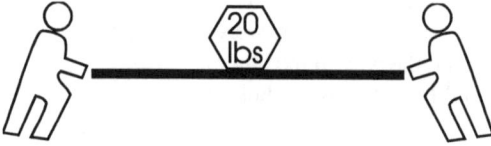

FIGURE 4   Anchoring example.
Question: How much does each man
have to push up to balance the 20-lb
load in the center of the board?

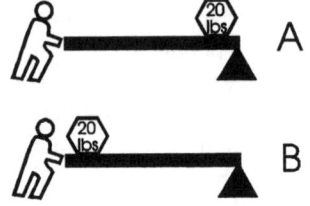

A

B

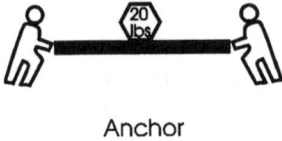

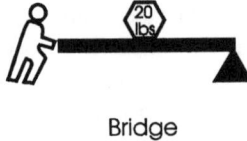

Anchor   Bridge

ANALOGICAL BRIDGING   EXTREME CASE COMPARISON

FIGURE 5   Initial lesson sequence.

agreement with accepted physical theory (Clement, Brown, & Zietsman, 1989),
was provided by the study's diagnostic tests.

Analogical bridging.   The bridging situation (illustrated in Figure 5) builds
on the students' belief that the two people shared the load in the anchoring example.
This sharing idea is extended analogically in the bridging example to a person and
a fulcrum sharing the load. (In both the anchor and the bridging examples, the
students were asked to estimate "how much of the load each person would hold.")

Initial extreme case.   A comparison between two extreme case situations was
presented at the end of the sequence to extend the ideas of sharing that may have
been triggered by the anchor and bridging situations. Students were asked to judge
which was the easier task of holding a 20-lb load, A or B, in Figure 5.

Introduction of terminology and extreme cases revisited.   In the earlier
exploratory tutoring sessions, the bridging sequence showed promise but was not
effective on its own in producing transferable conceptual change in most students.
A further problem was the emergence of an inert-objects-do-not-push (powerless-
objects) conception that prevented some students from accepting the analogy
between the anchoring and bridging cases. This conception is not compatible with
a physicist's view—students referred to the fulcrum as having "no power," that it
"cannot hold anything"—hence our term the *powerless-objects* conception. It is
most likely related to the *normal forces* alternative conceptions discussed in

Minstrell (1982) and Clement (1993). However, all the children responded with a useful physical intuition to the final extreme case comparison (in Figure 6). Hence, extreme cases were used more heavily in the lesson in this study.

The extreme case comparison from this sequence (see Figure 6a) was revisited after a short introduction to different terms, such as *lever arm* and *fulcrum*. A question was added to focus attention on the lever arms as variables ("Does it matter what the distance from the man to the load is?").

The second extreme cases comparison (see Figure 6b) drew attention to the relevant variables in an even more focused way. In this question, the load-effort separation distance (which turned out to be a distracter for most students) is kept constant, thus encouraging the children to reason in terms of the effort and load lever arms.

Participants and Procedure

Grade 7 students from one school participated in the systematic tutoring. All completed the diagnostics tests, and from the test results a list of students holding alternative conceptions in conflict with accepted physical theory were identified. From the list, a pool of students were selected by their teacher to represent three levels of ability with half boys and half girls. One student from each of these six subpools was assigned randomly to a tutoring group and to a control group. This means that a stratified sample of six students was interviewed in each of the two conditions discussed in this article.

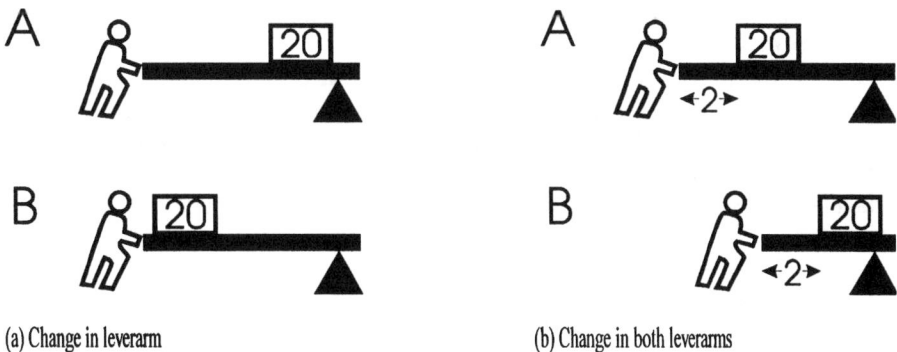

(a) Change in leverarm   (b) Change in both leverarms

FIGURE 6   Extreme cases revisited sequence.
Questions for each comparison:
1. Where would it be easier to keep the board with the 20-lb load on it level?
   (a) In Case A.
   (b) In Case B.
   (c) The same force would be needed to keep each board level.
2. Does it matter what the distance from the man to the load is?

Pre- and posttests were given before and after instruction for the experimental group. The same pre- and posttests were given on separate days without intervening instruction to a control group.

QUANTITATIVE RESULTS

Although the primary results discussed in this article are qualitative, a brief examination of prepost gains provides evidence for the overall effectiveness of the lessons. Scores were assigned to the students' answers and their confidence in the answers as follows: (a) positive and negative values to correct and wrong answers, respectively; (b) a number (1–4) to the confidence level (rated from a "guess" to "sure I'm right" on a 4-point scale); and (c) multiplying the confidence level number with the appropriate symbol to indicate a correct (or not) answer. Thus, a student who guessed a wrong answer would score –1 on a question, whereas a student who was sure that he or she was right about a wrong answer, would score –4. Gain scores as the difference between post- and prescores were calculated for each student and summed for each group. Using this method, the total score for the experimental group was 77 and the control group's was 5.

Although the numbers of students were small, the Mann–Whitney test was applied to the hypothesis that the control and experimental group were identical with respect to their gains on the pre- and posttests. Using a criterion ($p < .01$), the difference between groups was significant ($U = 4, p = .007$). This gives us an initial reason to believe that learning and conceptual change occurred during the treatment. (The Appendix gives the individual scores for the experimental and control group students.)

However, in this article we focus on an qualitative examination of transcripts for evidence of key learning episodes. Through such case study analyses, we may be able to make grounded hypotheses about the efficacy of particular methods and why they were effective. We restrict our attention to the first section of the lesson, that dealing with Class II levers. We begin these analyses in the next section.

TRANSCRIPT ANALYSES: EVIDENCE THAT LEARNING OCCURRED IN THE LEVERS LESSON

A Case Study Illustrating One Student's Learning Path

As an illustration of one student's reasoning, we present a protocol in Figure 7 providing evidence that learning occurred in the Class II levers lesson. (The preconception we have described as control conception is abbreviated "cc" in Figure 7.)

Lesson Element	Protocol Excerpt	Conception (inferred)

A. Analogical Bridging

Target

A
vs
B

| | 001
003 | ... B [easier] ... when
you're near the weight | C_c. |

Anchor

| | 017 | 10 lbs ... if they're each
pushing 10 lbs. then
together they push 20 lbs | share |

Bridge

| | 027
029 | I guess it's 10 lbs again?
... the thing [fulcrum]
hold the other ... 10 lbs up. | fulcrum
helps
model |

Extreme Case Comparison

A
vs
B

	043	... A, the weight is on this thing [fulcrum] resting on it?	fulcrum helps model
	044	But, here [B] he is holding the weight ... I think person B though ... [it is]	C_c.
	048	easier for him to keep the weight from moving the board.	C_c.

B. Extreme Cases Revisited

Comparison 1

A
vs
B

| | 200 | Ohhh. Well can I change
my mind ... if I answered
this [B] can I answer A? | Change |
| | 204 | ... the more the weight is
on the turning point, and
he's [a] holding less of it. | fulcrum-
helps
model |

Comparison 2

A
vs
B

| | 244 | [For B] the weight is almost
on the turning point so [he]
would not have to hold very
much of it ... | fulcrum-
helps
model |
| | 246 | ... because the turning point is
holding it up. | |

FIGURE 7   Protocol excerpts illustrating learning path for Student EE5.

Student EE5 used the control conception in her explanation for the preinstruction target question: She believed that a shorter Class II lever would make the task easier, because one would have more control over the load (line 005, Figure 7).

Initially, the analogical bridging sequence proceeded more or less as we intended: She was able to extend the anchoring example to the bridging situation and had apparently constructed the sharing model of the fulcrum intended (lines 017–029, Figure 7). However, her reasoning about the extreme case comparison situations in the bridging sequence regressed back to the control conception. This indicates that this new sharing conception is fragile and only applied in cases close to the anchor at first—it is in need of range extension and consolidation. She then used the control conception consistently until the second extreme case comparisons where she changed her mind (line 204, Figure 7). Her change of mind appeared to be abrupt, and it is apparent from the protocol that she is fully aware of this change.

This example provides evidence for learning that occurs during the time a participant is thinking about an extreme case. In line 204 (Figure 7), she responded with the correct answer and appeared to think in terms of a model of some of the weight being supported by the fulcrum, thereby reducing the effort. This is a very different conception from the control conception: There is evidence that she had considered her old way of thinking and a new way of thinking and that she preferred the new way, and that the new conception is applied later to other questions and used the following day on the posttest. The extreme case in line 200 appears to be a critical point in this protocol after which the student is able to overcome the control conception.

Other Patterns of Learning

The other students in the experimental group showed patterns of learning that are somewhat similar to that of Student EE5. Table 2 summarizes both the correctness of their answers (indicated by plus or minus signs) and the conceptions used (as inferred from the students' explanations) across the lesson:

c_c control conception

share   idea that the load is shared in the symmetrical anchoring and bridging examples

f-h   (fulcrum-helps model) explanatory model of the fulcrum's action in lever situations

c_{po} powerless-objects conception

c_l a conception with limited use—an explanation for one lever class only

TABLE 2
Maps of Students' Learning: Class II Levers Lesson

Student	Levers Lesson: Class II Levers					Posttest	
	Target	Anchor	Bridge	Extreme Cases	Target	Extreme Cases	Target
E1	− c_c	+ share model	+ share model	+ f-h model	− c_c	− c_c	− c_c
E2	+ c_i	+ share model	− c_{pc}	+ f-h model	+ f-h model	+ f-h model	+ f-h model
E3	− c_c	+ share model	− c_{po}	+ f-h model	− c_c	+ f-h model	+ f-h model
E4	− c_c	+ share model	+ f-h model	− c_c	− c_c	+ f-h model	+ f-h model
E5	− c_c	+ share model	+ f-h model	− c_c	− c_c	+ f-h model	+ f-h model
E6	+ c_i	− c_{po}	− c_{po}	+ share model	+ c_i	+ f-h model	+ f-h model

Note. See Table 1 for explanation of abbreviations.

There is evidence that all but one of the children had constructed more expert-like knowledge of levers by the end of the Class II levers lesson. The summary shows that most students started using more expert-like knowledge in an apparently consistent fashion from the first extreme cases comparison or the extreme cases revisited sequence onward. Although the anchor plus bridge appeared to facilitate temporary conceptual change in three students (EE1, EE4, and EE5), all reverted back to their preconceptions (or the powerless-objects conception) in the first extreme case comparison or in the postinstruction target question.

It appears therefore, from these maps of the children's progress during the lesson, that the extreme case situations were effective instructional components of the Class 2 levers lesson. The posttest target question was asked at the end of the 2-day-long intervention, and one can therefore not attribute the learning suggested in the posttest explanations to the extreme case components only. However, inspection of maps of students' explanations across the complete intervention shows that the first significant breakthrough for most students apparently occurred while considering the extreme case situations just described (Zietsman, 1991).

EVIDENCE ON HOW THE EXTREME CASES FOSTERED LEARNING: STUDENTS' CONSTRUCTION OF EXPLANATORY MODELS

In this section, we propose some hypotheses for why learning occurred as a result of the extreme case reasoning. For example, we present evidence that the extreme situations fostered the construction of an explanatory model that the fulcrum helps or supports some of the load in the lever situations. As an introduction to this discussion, we clarify our use of the term *explanatory model.*

Terms for Referring to Explanatory Models

The general term *mental model* is often used to denote a connected system of conceptions that produce declarative expectations about a certain target domain. We use the more specific term explanatory model as a particular type of mental model defined (with respect to a set of target situations to be explained) as

a conception of (schema for) a structure hidden in (not directly observable in) the target situation. It is intended to explain (and often predict) behavior patterns observable in the target. For example, the physicist can explain the law of levers by appealing to the model of forces and torques in a force diagram and torque diagram.

A number of scholars have argued that such explanatory models in science are distinguished from empirical laws that merely describe or summarize patterns of observations (Campbell, 1920; Harre, 1961; Hesse, 1966). Campbell's often cited example is that merely being able to make predictions from the empirical gas law, stating that PV is proportional to T in terms of macroscopic, measurable quantities, is not equivalent to understanding the theoretical explanation for gas behavior in terms of an imageable model of billiard-ball-like molecules in motion. Unlike the empirical law, the explanatory model provides a description of a hidden process that explains how the gas works and answers "why" questions about where observable changes in temperature and pressure come from. This qualitative model can also be extended and used as the foundation for a separate quantitative model that gives more detailed explanations and predictions.

In the view of Hesse (1966) and Harre (1961), scientific explanatory models are usually based on an analogy to a conception of a familiar situation. In our study, we hypothesize that these conceptions are physical intuitions based on perceptual motor schemas. A perceptual motor schema is a nonverbal interpretation and control structure that is active over a period of time and that assimilates, generates expectations about, and sometimes manipulates objects. Schmidt (1982) described such schemas (or "motor programs") as general in the sense that a single program can produce a large variety of responses depending on the values of certain input parameters. The perspective that a motor schema can have generality through a pattern of actions and expectations over time with parameters adjusted to a particular situation in a process of tuning has precedents in Piaget (1955), Neisser (1976), and Schmidt (1982). (By perceptual motor, we mean perceptual or motor or both. We use Schmidt's description then as one example of how such a schema might be general.) More details on this topic are given in Clement (1994a, 1994b).

We suggest that some explanatory models can be developed as students think about particular key instructional examples that activate certain useful physical intuitions of this kind. We define an intuitively anchored explanatory model as an explanatory model that is based on or constructed from a familiar schema. This can be considered to be a recursive definition. Perceptual motor schemas are assumed to be familiar in a primitive sense and can therefore serve as the anchor for a hierarchy of models. We suspect that intuitive anchoring is a desirable feature of explanatory models, which, among other things, makes them more memorable and helps give the student a feeling of conviction about them. For example, in the case of the anchor for levers, the intuition about two persons (at each end of the board) sharing the load in the center of the board is used to develop the model of the fulcrum supporting part of the load in a real lever. This is an explanatory model (albeit a very primitive one) because the students must project a hidden relation of force or support into the fulcrum. It is an intuitively anchored model because its origin is tied to a familiar schema—in this case a perceptual motor schema.

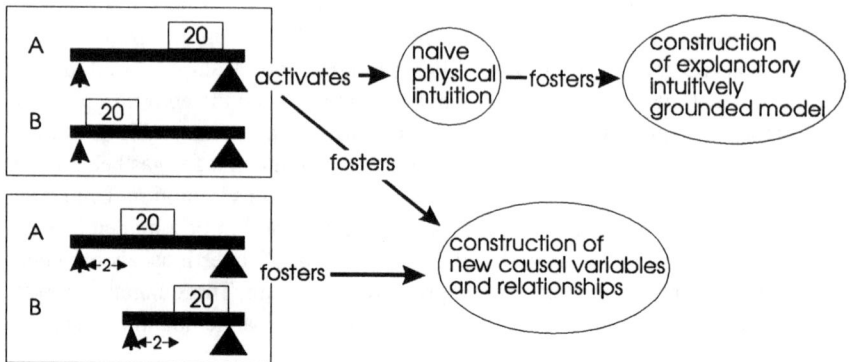

FIGURE 8   Learning facilitated by reasoning from extreme cases.

HOW LEARNING OCCURRED: REASONING FROM EXTREME CASES

In Figure 8, we outline hypotheses about ways in which the extreme case situations facilitated the construction of students' models (and thus new conceptions about the target situation).

The two major functions—the construction of an explanatory, intuitively anchored model and the construction of new causal variables—are now discussed.

Extreme Cases Fostered Model Construction

The intuition that was mentioned first by most students (when comparing the situations in Figure 8), is that Person B must "hold the whole 20 lb," an intuition probably informed by the children's prior experiences. Protocol examples of this kind of thinking are:

82   EE2:   This man is gonna have to do 20 lb in Case B.
             Cause it's [the load] right on him.

98   EE3:   I think here [B] the person would have to push
             all 20 lb.
100   Because it's [load] so close to him, that's
             where he has to hold it.

206   EE5:   Yeah, [A] has to push up less.
208   But this guy [B] is holding the whole 20 lb.

A second or "fulcrum-holds-more" intuition could be seen as related to the first intuition. The following protocol excerpts also illustrate the fulcrum-holding idea:

83	EE2:	And this man [A] will probably have to do 5 to 1 because it [the load] is so far away from him and the block is holding up most of the weight
111	EE3:	I think that this man [A] will [find it easier]. The weight is closer to the turning point and that might help keep it up a little.
76	EE4:	Person A [will find it easier], because the weight is closer to the triangle on this one.
77	I:	And what difference does that make?
78	EE4:	the triangle has more pressure on it.
202	EE5:	Well, I think it'll be easier for him [A]
204		The more the weight is on the turning point, and he is holding less of it.

It is surprising that this intuition was triggered by merely considering the extreme case examples, particularly because half of the students had declared a few minutes earlier that the fulcrum could not "hold any of the weight" in the bridging example. Why are they suddenly able to attribute such an action to the same object? We suggest that the extreme case activates a dormant support or sharing conception previously built up from experience.

We propose that all the students mentioned previously have constructed an explanatory, intuitively anchored model of the *fulcrum helping:* explanatory in the sense that the reduced effort is explained in terms of what is to the child a hidden function of the fulcrum helping (previously inert and not exerting a force) and anchored in the naive intuitions described earlier.

In contrast to explanatory models, an empirical rule predicts the behavior of a target by specifying a relation between observable features of the target. Siegler (1978) described children's ideas about a closely related device, the balance beam, in terms of empirical rules. For example, one simple but not always correct rule would be observed when children are considering only the weights on either side of the fulcrum. If the weights are the same, the system will balance—if not, the side with the greater weight will go down. Such a rule does not represent an explanatory model because it refers only to an association between two observable features.

Figure 9 illustrates a schematic way to think about the use of empirical rules and explanatory models in the levers context. Figure 9a shows a representation for an

(a)   Move load
       toward   ⟶ less
       EFFORT   effort

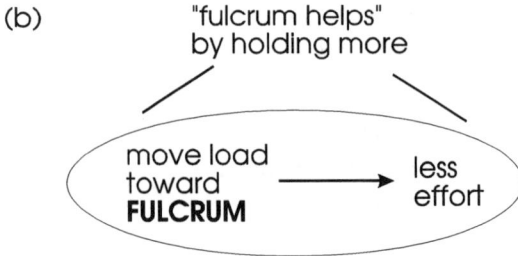

(b)   "fulcrum helps"
                 by holding more

       move load
       toward   ⟶ less
       FULCRUM   effort

FIGURE 9 Rules and models for levers.

empirical rule that refers only to a correlation between observable features. The "fulcrum helps by holding more" conception in Figure 9b can be thought of as an explanatory model because it refers to a nonobserved factor that provides more detail in the causal chain in the form of an intermediate, mediating, hidden mechanism. Although it is a rather primitive one, this is a model that the students can project into their view of the system. As such, it gives an explanation for why moving the load toward the fulcrum leads to a smaller effort on the part of the person.

In coming to view an idea this simple as an explanatory model we are stretching the use of the term explanatory model to include more primitive cases than in our previous usage (Brown & Clement, 1989). This perceptual motor schema is the simplest, most elementary example of an explanatory model that we have studied, and as such it is an attempt on our part to connect two ideas in philosophy of science and cognitive studies of children.

Using Extreme Cases to Construct New Causal Variables and Relations

Using a new variable.   In the pretest interviews, students focused strongly on a variable that experts ignore—the distance between the effort and the load. Students related the effort to the effort-load separation distance in two ways: (a) an increase in dEL results in a decreased effort and (b) a decrease in dEL results in a decreased effort.

We inferred from the protocols that the students were aware of, at most, the following variables before instruction: (a) the force exerted by the person, (b) the load, and (c) the effort-load separation distance. They never referred to the variable dLF (load-fulcrum distance) that is used by experts. Examples follow (the inferred variable is given at the end):

16	EE1:	because then the weight's closer to you.	load
		So, its probably easier to lift if	force
		the weight is closer to you.	dEL
14	EE2:	[B] ... because the weight of the 20 lb is	load
15		farther away from where you'd be holding it up	force
27	EE3:	[B] ... the weight is I guess	load
		closer to you	dEL
		maybe it's easier to hold	force
6	EE4:	[B] ... because you're closer to this [load]	load
			dEL
21	EE5:	[B] ... when you're closer to being underneath it	dEL
23		I think its easier to hold it	force
			load
5	EE6:	The man in A does not have to lift directly	force
		the 20 lb load	load
		[he] is lifting farther away from the 20 lb	dEL

The second comparison of lever situations involving extreme cases (Figure 8) was designed to initiate dissonance between the students' preinstruction connection of the effort-load separation distance and the magnitude of the effort required and the obviously crucial load arm differences in Cases A and B.

In addition, we had hoped that the fulcrum-helps model would be reinforced again. The last question was difficult for the children, because both lever arms are changed. The expectation was that they would rely on the fulcrum-helps model to explain Case B in particular—and this did happen. The students also focused on variables never mentioned before and constructed new relations between variables.

For example, Student EE3's reasoning about the preinstruction target question can be contrasted with her explanation for the extreme case comparisons (summarized in Figure 10).

The first extreme case comparison (lines 098–106, Figure 10) appears to lead her away from using a distracting variable (dEL). The result appears to be the formation of a new causal relation (i.e., the effort decreased; lines 102–104, Figure 10) because the load-fulcrum distance (dLF) decreased, as well as the application of a new variable, namely the load-fulcrum variable (dLF). This is the first time she has used this variable in a problem solution.

Lesson Element	Protocol Excerpt	Variables and Relationships

Extreme Case Comparison 1

$098E_3$:	I think here the person [B] would have to push 20 lbs	E >>
100	...because it's [load] so close to him.	d_{EL} <<
102	and here [A]... the person would have to push less.	E <<
104	it's [load] closer to the think	
105 I:	Closer to the?	
$106E_3$:	Closer to the turning point	d_{LF} <<

Extreme Case Comparison 2

$111E_3$:	[Easier for B]... because the weight is closer to the turning point and therefore that might keep it up a little.	E << d_{LF} << thus f-h
	Whereas this person [A], the dis-tance here is so far away	d_{LF} >>
112 I:	Distance from the load to the turning point you are pointing	
$113E_3$:	to?	
114 I:	Right, from the, ah, yeah.	
$115E_3$:	And what difference does that make? Well, I guess, ah, if it's (load) closer to the turning point then that might help keep it up.	d_{LF} << thus: f-h

FIGURE 10   Constructing new variables, constructing new relations.

In the second extreme case comparison (lines 111–115, Figure 10), the extreme case appears to not only draw out an intuition about the causal relation by providing a means for comparison but also the comparison encourages a focusing on the new (dLF) variable. In this example, the extreme case is used in combination with a second strategy of controlling for the distracting variable dEL. However, we saw that the new variable (dLF) actually was first applied in Comparison 1 for this student, in which no such control was used.

Five of the six students referred to the load-fulcrum distance (dLF) for the first time during an extreme case example in the instruction and four of these were in the second extreme case comparison only. It appears most likely that the role of the extreme case is to draw out the physical intuition that having the load close to the fulcrum shifts some of the job of support to the fulcrum. This interpretation is supported by the fact that all five students used the fulcrum-helps model. We conclude from such cases that it is possible for an extreme case to be an aid in the construction of a new variable.

Articulating a new relation.   In lines 111 and 115 (Figure 10), we see expressions close to a statement of a functional relation, such as: The closer the weight is to the fulcrum, the more it is supported by the fulcrum; for example, "because the weight is closer to the turning point and therefore that might keep it up a little" (line 111). These appear to emerge from the consideration of an extreme case.

In summary, we appear to have evidence for all three cognitive benefits of using an extreme case: the formation of new models, new variables, and new functional relations.

DISCUSSION

What Processes Underlie Learning From Extreme Cases?

In this section, we offer a theoretical interpretation for how extreme cases are fostering learning that is capable of explaining the case study data. The first possibility—the formally stated process given in the second section of this article on Extreme Case Reasoning—was: Such a relation can be inferred from the knowledge of two data points $(X0, Y0)$ and $(X1, Y1)$, and the assumption of a monotonic relation between the variables. However, the Grade 7 participants know nothing of monotonic functions, and therefore are almost certainly not deducing conclusions in this rigorous fashion.

A somewhat less formal view of extreme case reasoning is as follows: Participants possess information in long-term memory that allows them to look up an episodic memory of a an extreme case as a prior event in their experience (data point). They can then compare this memory to that of an ordinary case with respect to the two (presumably causally related) variables X and Y. Monotonicity takes the form of a natural, implicit assumption that simply amounts to trying the simplest relation first. In the case of levers, these causally related variables may be distance of the load from the fulcrum and force of effort required. The comparison leads to an ordinal relation of the form: An increase in A leads to an increase in B.

Schema activation leading to an ordinal function.   However, we suspect that our students' conclusions have a more meaningful and direct semantic basis than the look up of memorized data points. We hypothesize that the drawing of the weight at the extreme, as near to the fulcrum as possible, activates a support schema, helping schema, or both as applied to the fulcrum. Such a schema allows a primitive form of mental simulation to occur in which the participant can imagine having to exert less force on the other end of the board. The activation of a general schema means that this can in effect take place as a thought experiment, without the participant needing to have a particular episodic memory of the situation shown in the drawing. It may be that a monotonic function is present implicitly in the students' perceptual motor schema that generates the new simulation of the situation. That is, the rough, qualitative, functional relation is embodied in the schema itself and is an emergent feature of its activity. (A simpler example is that an estimator for "how hard to lift" is built into schema for picking up objects: The larger the object, the larger the force that is needed; Mounoud & Bower, 1974.) Once the extreme case triggers the helping or supporting schema, that provides a direct way of simulating the situation that is capable of providing implicit information that can be described explicitly by the statement that the closer the load is to the turning point, the more it will help to support it.

Formation of a new variable.   The activation of this schema makes the fulcrum the new reference point for describing the position of the load, allowing the closeness to the fulcrum to become a variable. This then allows the construction of a new relation in terms of this variable. The following are the subprocesses we see as consistent with the transcript of E3 in Figure 10 just discussed.

1. Activating one or more perceptual motor schemas for helping or supporting, as applied to the fulcrum supporting part of the block. In our terms, this provides a primitive new explanatory model of a hidden influence in the situation.
2. The student uses the schema to simulate comparisons of values of effort for the extreme case in comparison with another case.
3. The schema also encourages the student to focus on a new variable.
4. The student is then capable of expressing a new ordinal relation in terms of the new variable.

This set of subprocesses also appears to be consistent with EE5's transcript in Figure 7. It provides an initial account for how the three identified benefits of extreme case reasoning are realized together in these transcripts. In this view, we have emphasized the idea of an *explanatory model*—the activation of a schema that interprets situations and projects imagined elements into it—rather than the idea of an algorithm for inferring a relation from two pairs of data points. The hypothesized process is *more complex than a simple look-up algorithm* in the following ways:

1. One of the variables has not previously been defined or even attended to by the participant, and this variable may need to be isolated explicitly and defined. (One way this could happen is if information in an analog representation is converted to linguistic information.)

2. This is consistent with the view that a perceptual motor schema may be the source of the physical intuition used in these extreme cases. Such schemas can

embody implicit functions to vary expectations and actions in accord with different situations (Schmidt, 1982).

3. The idea of the fulcrum helping is the participant's semantic interpretation of it—a meaning that he or she projects into the situation—as opposed to just an algorithm for calculation or the memory of an event.

4. The participants do not mention values of force or data points for the extreme cases. This supports the view that their comprehension of the ordinal relation between distance from the fulcrum and weight supported by the fulcrum is very direct, rather than an inference from two known data points.

5. The entire inference in this view is dependent on the perceptual motor schema. Such schemas may be quite different from a list of facts (see Clement, 1994a, 1994b; Neisser, 1976; Schmidt, 1982).

Extreme cases as schema activators.   The following question remains: Why was this schema not activated by the nonextreme cases? The answer to this question may be related to the small domain size of naive conceptions noted by diSessa (1985). The range of situations that activate this and many more of the naive student's conceptions is either displaced from or simply much narrower than that of the expert scientist. Our task then becomes helping students to extend the activation range of the positive intuitions they have (in agreement with the physicist) from intuitive extreme case or anchoring situations to other more difficult situations. This is a major strategy taken in these lessons.[1]

CONCLUSIONS

Roles for Extreme Cases

The purpose of this article was to use qualitative analyses of tutoring transcripts as an empirical base to develop models for thinking about the roles and mechanisms that can make extreme cases a powerful learning tool. We began with the question of how extreme cases may be used for more than a check in simple problem solutions by playing a role in students' learning. We have confirmed that one role of extreme cases is to provide a firm comparison that helps one to establish a causal, direction-of-change relation (ordinal function) between two given variables. We have also identified two new roles for extreme cases in fostering learning, namely:

---

[1]In other cases, the schema may already be activated by the original problem. The extreme case may then serve as a situation that provides a clear contrast for a mental simulation using the schema—one that draws out implicit knowledge in a clear and unambiguous way with high confidence. The central view of extreme cases working by drawing implicit knowledge out of an existing schema remains the same.

(a) their role in activating a perceptual motor schema that is used to construct an explanatory model and (b) their role in contributing to the formation of new causal variables. In the case studies, these processes appear to be prerequisites for the desired role of forming and articulating a new ordinal relation. Pending confirmation of similar effects in another subject area, these roles are candidates for being included in a set of general learning strategies for science instruction.

These two additional mechanisms for learning via extreme cases add support to the following hypothesis. The conceptual change facilitated by this instructional sequence did not simply consists of the formulation or confirmation of a statement of the form: A causes an increase in B. Rather, it includes the construction of a new way of seeing lever situations in the sense that the students (a) are sensitive to new concepts or features of levers that they did not see earlier and (b) are able to imagine a hidden visualizable explanatory mechanism and project it into lever situations. This knowledge restructuring resembles the strong conceptual change requirements of Carey (1986) and Vosniadou and Brewer (1987): (a) the construction of new core conceptions, (b) establishment of new relations between conceptions, and (c) explanation of a different domain of phenomenon. We have provided some evidence for this, although it is debatable whether the students' introduction of the fulcrum as a significant, new element of the levers can be construed as evidence of the third requirement.

How Extreme Cases Lead to New Knowledge

We have hypothesized, on the basis of transcript data, that many extreme cases work by making it possible to tap implicit knowledge in perceptual motor schemas as the source of physical intuition involved. This view contrasts with views of extreme case knowledge as episodic memories and with more formal views of algorithms for making inferences from data points. In this article, we have provided some empirical support for the view of the role of extreme cases as activating flexible perceptual motor schemas, as a process prior to the formation of verbal rules (e.g., more A means more B). This view is very compatible with Nersessian's (1992) speculation that extreme cases in the history of science involve mental simulations in a thought experiment. It helps explain how students appeared to make breakthroughs from thinking about one or two examples rather than having to look for a pattern of observable events in many examples.

Implications for Teaching

The use of extreme cases and explanatory models of hidden mechanisms have been much more powerful teaching strategies than we had expected for this younger age group. We were surprised by these results because these strategies often appeared to be more powerful than the analogical reasoning techniques we were counting on originally. Surprises like these testify to the power of descriptive, learning-aloud studies to criticize and improve teaching strategies.

Implied recommendations for curriculum development and teaching from this study are the following:

1. Draw out and listen to students' naive explanations to identify their preconceptions that conflict with the scientist's conceptions.

2. Use extreme cases as one way to tap positive preconceptions in students that agree with the scientist's view.

3. Investigate (in our case, in a research project) whether extreme cases have been chosen, so that they actually do activate schemas in students that allow them to make accurate predictions. A strong finding from our study is that one cannot assume that whatever makes sense to the teacher or researcher will also make sense to students.

4. Investigate whether students are seeing or attending to the same variables that the teacher or researcher are in the proposed situations.

5. Temporary, intuitively worded labels for variables, such as *load arm* and *turning point,* may help this process.

6. Design some extreme cases to create dissonance with alternative conceptions.

7. Allow time for and support the process of converting case comparisons into general statements of qualitative functions of the form: Increasing A leads to an increase in B.

Further Research Needed

There are a number of questions we have not been able to address with this data, such as: Now that we have some models for thinking about the roles and mechanisms that make extreme cases important in learning, can we design an experiment showing that when important extreme case examples are replaced by ordinary examples, less learning occurs? How do experts and students pick good extreme cases? Because many possible extreme cases could be generated, how do experts, teachers, and students pick the best one for a given circumstance? Sometimes an extreme case moves the example too far by moving it into a regime that behaves very differently from the intended problem. How do people evaluate whether the inferences they make from extreme cases are valid? These are among the many interesting questions for future work in this area.

REFERENCES

Brown, D., & Clement, J. (1989). Overcoming misconceptions via analogical reasoning: Abstract transfer versus explanatory model construction. *Instructional Science, 18,* 237–261.

Campbell, N. (1920). *Physics: The elements.* Cambridge, England: Cambridge University Press.

Carey, S. (1986). Cognitive science and science education. *American Psychologist, 41,* 1123–1130.

Clement, J. (1988). Observed methods for generating analogies in scientific problem solving. *Cognitive Science, 12,* 563–586.

Clement, J. (1989). Learning via model construction and criticism: Protocol evidence on sources of creativity in science. In J. Glover, R. Ronning, & C. Reynolds (Eds.), *Handbook of creativity: Assessment, theory and research* (pp. 341–381). New York: Plenum.

Clement, J. (1991). Nonformal reasoning in experts and in science students: The use of analogies, extreme cases, and physical intuition. In J. Voss, D. Perkins, & J. Siegel (Eds.), *Informal reasoning and education* (pp. 345–362). Hillsdale, NJ: Lawrence Erlbaum Associates, Inc.

Clement, J. (1993). Using bridging analogies and anchoring intuitions to deal with students' preconceptions in physics. *Journal of Research in Science Teaching, 30,* 1241–1257.

Clement, J. (1994a). Imagistic simulation and physical intuition in expert problem solving. In *Proceedings of the Sixteenth Annual Meeting of the Cognitive Science Society* (pp. 201–206). Hillsdale, NJ: Lawrence Erlbaum Associates, Inc.

Clement, J. (1994b). Use of physical intuition and imagistic simulation in expert problem solving. In D. Tirosh (Ed.), *Implicit and explicit knowledge* (pp. 204–244). Norwood, NJ: Ablex.

Clement, J., Brown, D., & Zietsman, A. (1989). Not all preconceptions are misconceptions: Finding "anchoring" conceptions for grounding instruction on students' intuitions. *International Journal of Science Education, 11,* 554–565.

diSessa, A. (1985). Knowledge in places. In G. Forman & P. Pufall (Eds.), *Constructivism in the computer age* (pp. 49–70). Hillsdale, NJ: Lawrence Erlbaum Associates, Inc.

Galileo, G. (1954). *Two new sciences* (H. Crew & A. de Salvio, Trans.). Toronto, Canada: Dover. (Original work published in 1638)

Harre, R. (1961). *Theories and things.* London: Newman History and Philosophy of Science Series.

Hesse, M. (1966). *Models and analogies in science.* South Bend, IN: Notre Dame University Press.

Minstrell, J. (1982). Explaining the "at rest" condition of an object. *The Physics Teacher, 20,* 10–14.

Mounoud, P., & Bower, T. G. R. (1974). Conservation of weight in infants. *Cognition, 3,* 29–40.

Neisser, U. (1976). *Cognition and reality.* San Francisco: Freeman.

Nersessian, N. J. (1989). Conceptual change in science and science education. *Synthese, 80,* 163–183.

Nersessian, N. J. (1992). How do scientists think? Capturing the dynamics of conceptual change in science. In R. Giere (Ed.), *Minnesota studies in the philosophy of science: Vol. 15. Cognitive models of science* (pp. 3–44). Minneapolis: University of Minnesota Press.

Piaget, J. (1955). *The child's construction of reality.* London: Routledge & Kegan Paul.

Polya, G. (1954). *Mathematics and plausible reasoning: Vol 1. Induction and analogy in mathematics.* Princeton, NJ: Princeton University Press.

Schmidt, R. A. (1982). *Motor control and learning.* Champaign, IL: Human Kinetics.

Siegler, R. S. (1978). The origins of scientific reasoning. In R. S. Siegel (Ed.), *Children's thinking: What develops?* (pp. 109–149). Hillsdale, NJ: Lawrence Erlbaum Associates, Inc.

Vosniadou, S., & Brewer, W. F. (1987). Theories of knowledge restructuring in development. *Review of Educational Research, 57,* 51–67.

Weld, D. (1990). Exaggeration. *Artificial Intelligence, 43,* 311–368.

Zietsman, A. I. (1991). *Case studies of cycles in developing a physics lesson.* Unpublished doctoral dissertation, University of Massachusetts, Amherst.

Zietsman, A. I., & Hewson, P. W. (1986). Effect of instruction using microcomputer simulations and conceptual change strategies on science learning. *Journal of Research in Science Teaching, 23,* 27–39.

APPENDIX
Experimental and Control Groups: Pre- and Postgain Scores

Experimental Group Gain		Control Group Gain	
Student	Summed Score	Student	Summed Score
EE1	+12	C1	+ 4
EE2	+21	C2	0
EE3	+16	C3	0
EE4	+ 1	C4	+14
EE5	+18	C5	− 6
EE6	+ 9	C6	− 7
Group total	+77	Group total	+ 5

THE JOURNAL OF THE LEARNING SCIENCES, 6(1), 91–142

Dynamic Science Assessment: A New Approach for Investigating Conceptual Change

Shirley J. Magnusson and Mark Templin
Educational Studies
The University of Michigan

Robert A. Boyle
Graduate School of Education
Fordham University

Starting from the premise that understanding conceptual change requires studying it while it occurs, this article describes a new research methodology in which students' knowledge is assessed in the context of mediated learning situations that attempt to foster conceptual change. The methodology builds on two ideas: that conceptual change in science is a matter of appropriation by individuals of culturally based knowledge (of the scientific community), and that understanding such change requires a mediated context in which the students' activity (actions and thinking) is shaped by a more experienced other who reflects the cultural norms or ideals of the scientific community that facilitate knowledge production. Specific assessments developed with these ideas in mind, which we call *dynamic science assessments* (DSAs), function to determine students' potential to change their understanding and as a result inform us about the process of conceptual change toward scientific knowledge. Results of a DSA about electricity that we conducted with upper elementary school children (*n* = 28) indicated that it was possible to foster conceptual change and to discriminate children with respect to their *potential* to develop scientifically accurate conceptions of current and resistance. These findings indicate the promise of using mediated learning situations, such as a DSA to study conceptual change in science, and we discuss the direction of future work given the conservative mediation in the assessments conducted in this particular instance.

Requests for reprints should be sent to Shirley J. Magnusson, 1323 SEB, 610 East University, Ann Arbor, MI 48109–1259 E-mail: smag@umich.edu

The question of conceptual change has been prominent in studies of science learning over the last 15 years as researchers strove to understand results from many studies examining children's explanations of natural phenomena. Although some researchers have discussed the theoretical and methodological differences among studies (e.g., Confrey, 1990; Driver & Easley, 1978; Driver & Erickson, 1983; Gilbert & Watts, 1983), the tendency has been to draw broad generalizations across this body of research (e.g., Wandersee, Mintzes, & Novak, 1994). These generalizations—such as the assertion that when students do not have the same ideas as scientists those ideas need to be replaced—have been criticized on the grounds that they are inconsistent with a constructivist epistemology (J. P. Smith, diSessa, & Roschelle, 1993). This criticism suggests the need to reexamine our conceptions and investigations of conceptual change. Our work does so in building from a different theoretical base than previous studies aiming to understand conceptual change—a sociocultural view of cognition. This view is constructivist in nature; however, it is markedly different from cognitive constructivist orientations to learning that focus within the individual, and as such requires the use of different tools to understand conceptual change. In this article, we present our view of conceptual change from a sociocultural frame and describe a new tool for assessing it, as well as results from our work with elementary school students in a study of conceptual change in the topic area of electricity.

THE NATURE OF KNOWLEDGE AND CONCEPTUAL CHANGE

A fundamental issue in the study of conceptual change is the conception of knowledge that underlies the investigation. We assume that an individual's knowledge can be meaningfully represented in terms of *concepts*, as is implied in the term *conceptual change*, and we describe our perspective of knowledge by drawing on previous and emerging ideas concerning the nature of concept. This perspective is used to describe our view of the nature of conceptual change in science learning.

Views of Concept

Gilbert and Watts (1983) identified at least three views of concept underlying research concerning learning science. One view, a traditional view of concept referred to as the *classical* view, depicts knowledge as comprised of entities (concepts) that are defined by some number of properties that are necessary and sufficient to distinguish them from other entities (E. E. Smith & Medin, 1981). Concepts are assumed to fit together in a hierarchical scheme, but each remains separate and distinct and can be studied independently. A similar but more elaborate characterization of knowledge is the *relational* view. In this view, concepts are defined by the relations or links between them, and the structure of the knowledge they represent is not restricted to a hierarchy. Concepts are pictured as forming a web or a network (e.g., Anderson, 1983), and some theories contend that a change in some element of the network can influence many or all other elements in the web.

A relational view of concept is implicit in many expert–novice studies in which the structure of conceptions of novices are compared to experts (e.g., Chi, Feltovich, & Glaser, 1981). Such comparisons often lead to deficiency rather than efficacy models of learners; that is, representing learners in terms of what they cannot do or what they do not know compared to experts (Metz, 1995). In addition, this view may underlie the thinking of those who attribute theory-like behavior to children's concepts (e.g., McCloskey, 1983), in contrast to others who suggest that the components of knowledge, although interconnected, are likely distributed across a variety of domains and range from general to context specific (e.g., diSessa, 1988; J. P. Smith et al., 1993). J. P. Smith et al. argued that a deficit perspective overemphasizes the differences and underemphasizes the similarities between experts and novices, thereby misrepresenting the issue of conceptual change. The research of Clement, Brown, and Zietsman (1989) is illustrative because it has focused on helping students build from their ideas that are accurate with respect to experts, even though they may have other ideas that are contrary (a common occurrence in the domain in which they have worked: mechanics). Results of their research provides evidence that conceptual change can occur gradually and without focusing on the replacement of existing conceptions.

Another perspective of concepts is the *actional* view. In contrast to the classical and relational views in which the state of one's conceptual knowledge is primarily static, this view represents knowledge as dynamic in nature. According to Gilbert and Watts (1983), an actional perspective "presents concepts as active, constructive and intentional" (p. 66), such as reflected in Neisser's description that conceptualizing is a "kind of doing" or Freyberg and Osborne's contention that even though concepts help us organize our experiences they do not remain unchanged with new experiences. Rather, Freyberg and Osborne contend that "all cognitive learning involves some degree of re-conceptualizing our existing knowledge" (as cited in Gilbert & Watts, 1983, p. 66).

This dynamic characteristic sets this perspective apart from the other views of concept, and the metaphor of a flame (Piattelli-Palmarini, 1980) is useful in conveying how this conception can account for the characterizations of knowledge resident in the other views and yet provide different ideas as well. First, if we imagine a candle flame, we know that it can appear stable and can seem to be a single entity just as concepts are viewed in static terms in the other views. Second, despite the apparent stability of a flame, we know it arises from continuously interacting substances just as the relational view of concept recognizes the importance of the connections among concepts. Third, the existence and stability of the flame is dependent on its surroundings, without oxygen there would be no flame, and the movement of air around a candle can make the flame waver. We consider this feature of the metaphor to represent the issue of context in learning, which is not indicated in the classical or relational views of concept. We suggest that an actional view implies that context is critical to understanding knowledge and learning, and in that way it is compatible with views of learning influenced by a sociocultural view of cognition.

Learning in sociocultural terms is fundamentally about context because all learning is viewed as situated (e.g., Brown, Collins, & Duguid, 1989); that is, learning is a function of the nature of the social context in which learning occurs. Moreover, the social context is considered to be fundamentally an expression of cultural norms and expectations operating in specific situations. Thus, cognition is not only a function of the social context but also the cultural environment framing that context. In the words of Lave (1988):

> There is reason to suspect that what we call cognition is in face a complex social phenomenon. The point is not so much that arrangements of knowledge in the head correspond in a complicated way to the social world outside the head, but that they are socially organized in such a fashion as to be indivisible. "Cognition" observed in everyday practice is distributed—stretched over, not divided among—mind, body, activity and culturally organized settings which include other actors. (p. 1)

The notion of *conceptual profile* helps to illustrate what these ideas mean with respect to the nature of knowledge and its development.

Concept as Conceptual Profile

Drawing on the work of Bachelard (1940/1968), the idea of a conceptual profile is that individuals can have parallel conceptions with respect to a specific concept, each conception having functionality within a particular social context (Solomon, 1983). In sociocultural terms, we would say that parallel conceptions develop because a concept that is sufficient to perceive and understand in one social context and with respect to one culture may not suffice in another. On the other hand, parallel conceptions can also be useful in the same cultural context if they are useful for perceiving or understanding in a particular activity. For example, Driver, Asoko, Leach, Mortimer, and Scott (1994) have argued that a chemist may reasonably have at least three conceptions of a solid: a quantum view, an atomistic view, and a continuous view. Whereas a quantum view reflects theory currently accepted by the scientific community and is one that would be necessary to employ to construct meaning and knowledge from the work of fellow chemists, an atomistic view could be useful in other activity that is part of the chemist's scientific practice. In contrast, in an everyday context it is far simpler and generally sufficient to employ a continuous view of solids, and doing so would be critical to being able to participate in the activities of one's everyday communities, such as when conversing with one's neighbor about good practice in winterizing a house.

The scientist in this example uses different conceptions in her scientific practice than in her everyday life because the community standards that dictate expectations for knowledge production and use in scientific practice are different from those guiding our everyday thinking. We can consider the different conceptions of solids as representing three of four levels at which one can construct understanding according to Bachelard (1968). Each level functions as a frame of reference for thinking, and the levels differ with respect to their degree of generality and explanatory power. Mortimer (1995) argued that the epistemological and ontological differences between the levels means that it is possible to learn a concept at a particular level without reference to less complex levels. Chi (1991) similarly argued that conceptual development "across" ontological categories is not properly called conceptual change because concepts develop within an ontological "tree"; initial conceptions from the initial ontological tree remain intact, and it only appears that a radical change has occurred because the outcome is that a new type of entity (ontologically) has developed. These ideas lead us to suggest that conceptual change involves the development of knowledge guided by particular ontological and epistemological assumptions. In contrast to our everyday knowledge building, developing scientific knowledge will require a radical shift in perspective or *frame of reference* from the cultural norms guiding our thinking in everyday life to those that guide knowledge production in the scientific community.

The notion that conceptual change refers to changes in specific ideas as well as epistemological commitments, ontological commitments, or both, is not new. Indeed, it is reflected in the construct of a conceptual ecology, which was advanced by Posner, Strike, Hewson, and Gertzog (1982) in a seminal article describing conceptual change in science learning. An important difference in our view, given the notion of conceptual profile, is that an individual can construct meaning and understanding from multiple perspectives that differ along epistemological or ontological dimensions or both. Thus, we do not presume that an individual must develop or adopt a way of thinking and knowing consistent with the culture of science as a singular way of being. We presume that individuals who are scientifically literate are able to operate from appropriate epistemological and ontological assumptions and access appropriate knowledge when participating in activity requiring the cultural stance of science; other assumptions and knowledge will be brought to bear in different contexts that require other stances. Just as individuals can learn to participate meaningfully within different ethnic cultures, we submit that students can learn to participate meaningfully within different academic cultures. To understand how this outcome is possible, we turn to a sociocultural construct called the zone of proximal development (ZPD), which depicts a process in which students learn science by being engaged in culturally relevant activity with respect to scientific practice, and are supported to develop competence in such activity.

The ZPD

The idea of the ZPD originated with the Russian theorist Vygotsky (1978), a psychologist who articulated a sociohistorical theory of development. In the words of Newman, Griffin, and Cole (1989), Vygotsky's view of psychology was that it concerned

> the dialectic between the inter- and the intra-psychological and the transformations of one into another. Mind becomes externalized by a culture in its tools, such as written language and social institutions. Cognitive change involves internalizations and transformations of the social relations in which children are involved, including the cultural tools which mediate the interactions among people and between people and the physical world. (p. 60)

Vygotsky invented the ZPD as a way to represent the influence of the social world on cognitive development. Generally, a ZPD can be defined as an "interactive system" formed by at least two individuals as the result of working on a problem which at least one of them could not effectively solve alone (p. 61). The "zone" is created as the participants engage in appropriate activity to develop shared understanding of the problem and work through a solution. In this process, the more expert individual (e.g., a teacher) changes cognitively as he or she develops understanding of the perspective of the other individual (and perhaps the problem and its solution as well), and the individual with less expertise (e.g., a student) changes cognitively through the process of coming to learn how to solve the problem, albeit with the assistance of the more expert individual. Development, in this view, is driven by improved performance. As described by Newman et al. (1989):

> Children can participate in an activity that is more complex than they can understand, producing "performance before competence," to use Cazden's (1981) phrase. While in the ZPD of an activity, the children's actions get interpreted within the system being constructed with the teacher. Thus the child is exposed to the teacher's understanding without necessarily being directly taught. (pp. 63–64)

It is also important to understand that the activity in which the individuals engage to form a ZPD is culturally specific. As a result, the ZPD can be conceived of as a "fundamentally functional system for cognitive change" (Newman et al., 1989, p. 71) because the context is intended to support the appropriation of tools (intellectual and material) of a particular culture, and the appropriation of tools assumes "adopting the belief system of the culture in which they are used" (Brown et al., 1989, p. 33).

With regard to conceptual change—that is, conceptual development within particular epistemological and ontological categories—we submit that it can be fostered through the establishment of ZPDs in which the culture of science is reflected. The next section describes our ideas about how to conceptualize the ideals of the scientific community for the purpose of guiding students' activity to foster the development of scientific knowledge.

Scientific Activity and Standards of Scientific Knowledge Production

Scientists are generally thought of as being concerned with studying the natural world to describe and explain it. From the standpoint of the scientific community, however, "the objects of science are not the phenomena of nature but constructs that are advanced by the scientific community to interpret nature" (Driver et al., 1994, p. 5). Using the metaphor of "tools" as is common in the sociocultural literature, we find it useful to characterize the practice of science as concerning the construction, use, and evaluation of tools (material and intellectual) that guide physical and mental activity in investigating nature. The intellectual tools developed for explanatory purposes are expected to fit particular standards, such as consistency, coherence, and completeness (J. P. Smith et al., 1993, describing the view of Einstein, 1950). Thus, scientific explanations are expected to be able to be usefully applied in multiple contexts (consistency), they are expected to fit together with respect to one another (coherence), and they are ultimately expected to contribute to a complete explanation of a particular aspect of the physical world (completeness).

The norms guiding knowledge building within any one area of science, however, include additional expectations that are more content specific than these standards. For example, what counts as a viable explanation of a particular phenomenon will be dictated by the views of the members of the scientific community who typically study that phenomenon. Those views are a consequence of knowledge, experience, and beliefs regarding previous explanations that were ventured to explain the phenomenon of interest and that gained community support. Thus, development with respect to specific scientific knowledge requires attention to domain-specific and domain-general norms.

The importance of these ideas is to reiterate that the expectations guiding our everyday thinking are quite different from those guiding scientific knowledge building. Our everyday explanations for phenomena are not expected to fit multiple contexts, and they are not commonly subjected to systematic empirical verification. In studies of science learning, unless it was clearly signaled to students that their descriptions and explanations should adhere to the standards of the scientific community, we expect them to employ the frames of reference used in their everyday sense making. As a result, it should not surprise us that many studies revealed students' everyday knowledge, and that it is radically different from scientific knowledge. We should not, however, presume that this result informs us sufficiently about students' development of scientific knowledge. Indeed, even scientists have been found to revert to commonsense notions and make inaccurate predictions when confronted with everyday problems, even though they could have used scientific knowledge in their area of expertise (e.g., chemists: Lewis & Linn, in press; physicists: McDermott, 1984). Thus, if we are to determine the scientific knowledge that individuals have or can develop, we must signal the standards by which knowledge is to be applied in sense-making and knowledge construction.

We argue that this has not been a feature of the methodologies employed to examine conceptual change, and as a result, we may have been mislead about the issues confronting students in the construction of scientific knowledge. Our work has attempted to address this issue by developing a different approach to assessing learning in which the expectations of the scientific community are reflected in the context. Before describing the principles guiding this approach, we end this section by describing our view of conceptual change.

A Sociocultural View of Conceptual Change in Science

Some sociocultural theorists use the term *cognitive change* to "characterize a process involving a dialectical interaction between the social world and the changing individual" (Newman et al., 1989, p. 59). This type of change involves "the internalization and transformation of the social relations in which individuals are involved, including the cultural tools which mediate the interactions among people and between people and the physical world" (Newman et al., 1989, p. 60). We hold a similar view regarding conceptual change. Using the context of establishing a zone of proximal development, we view conceptual change as a process that involves a dialectical interaction in which one individual, using psychological and material tools reflective of the activity of science (one aspect of the social world), supports another individual in using language and performing actions that represent appropriate ways of engaging the world from the perspective of the scientific community. The conceptual change that results from this type of interaction over time is the gradual development of knowledge that is marked by epistemological and ontological features consistent with that of practicing scientists. Whereas this development may appear to result in radically different knowledge from the everyday ideas individuals hold, it should not be viewed as a change to different ideas because the initial conceptions remain and are useful in many nonscientific contexts. Instead, it should be viewed as the evolution of ideas within particular ontological and epistemological categories, which results in the development of parallel conceptions that can be expressed in a conceptual profile (Mortimer, 1995). In addition, whereas we depict this change as evolutionary rather than revolutionary, that it not to say that the change is easy, unproblematic, or occurs readily. Operating within a ZPD assumes that the learning outcome is proximal to the initial knowledge of the learner; hence, development will occur in small steps. Furthermore, in the case of developing knowledge within a different ontological or epistemological category, difficult challenges may arise if individuals have few ideas or experiences to support knowledge construction. It is fair to describe this as a process of enculturation, and as such it will take time, errors will occur, and individual differences may mean that conceptual development will look very different across individuals.

To study such development, our challenge is to determine, in particular contexts, how to establish a zone of proximal development with material and psychological tools that are reflective of the activity of scientists and are facilitative in supporting improved performance. This view presupposes a very different context for investigating conceptual change, which we describe in specific terms in the next section.

INVESTIGATING CONCEPTUAL CHANGE

Many studies of science learning have employed rather static approaches to assessing understanding, focusing on end states rather than instances of change. We suggest that one reason such methods have mislead us in characterizing conceptual change in revolutionary terms is that they have typically provided "snapshots" rather than "movies" of development (Siegler & Crowley, 1991). With snapshots, it may appear that a conception cannot be constructed from the initial understanding, whereas movies may reveal ways in which it can, especially in contexts that promote the epistemological and ontological frames of reference that guide scientific practice. Developmental psychologists who have long been interested in understanding change and the mechanisms that produce it advocate use of the "microgenetic" method to study development. Siegler and Crowley (1991) described three attributes that distinguish this method from other approaches: (a) a change is observed from its beginning to a stable point, (b) there are a large number of observations relative to the rate of change, and (c) analyses attend to qualitative as well as quantitative aspects of a change.

These attributes indicate that investigating conceptual change requires a context in which change occurs rather than contexts that mark points between which change occurs and from which inferences are drawn about the change. Moreover, in the words of Inhelder and colleagues, the most appropriate method should "permit the subject to have the opportunity for repeated learning experiences to activate his existing schemes and to increase the opportunity for interaction between these schemes and the emergent schemes which result from interaction with the problem environment" (as cited in Siegler & Crowley, 1991, p. 608). We argue that establishing and working within a ZPD provides just such a context.

Some may consider this position to be antithetical to appropriate research practice; to intervene and support students in developing knowledge would seem to invalidate one's data. To the contrary, Smagorinsky (1995) argued that to assume that the study of learning can take place outside the bubble of the social environment of learning is to misconceptualize the role of mediation in human development and to underestimate the effects of the introduction of any research tools into the learning environment. (p. 205)

Thus, we argue that we have all along been prompting learning by asking students to complete particular tasks in our assessments of understanding. If that is the case, let us be purposeful in promoting learning for the purpose of studying conceptual change.

Approaches to Investigating Change Within a ZPD

Establishing a ZPD provides the participants with opportunities to develop their conceptions. The degree of change resulting from a particular interaction will be a function of the extent to which the zone moves due to the willingness and ability of the student participant to respond to scaffolding by the experienced participant, and the extent to which the experienced participant can provide scaffolding that is functional for the student participant. That requires finding or developing appropriate problems so that participants can construct a ZPD through engagement in culturally relevant activities. If the nature of the problem is too far above or too far below the actual development of the child, the participants will not be able to form a ZPD.

This type of approach has been employed in studies of cognitive development and is referred to as *dynamic assessment.*

Dynamic Assessment

Dynamic assessment is a phrase coined by Feuerstein, who is generally credited with originating the idea of this approach. These assessments are distinguishable from other approaches to assessing individual performance in that the participants (e.g., researcher and student) interact in a guided learning situation in which the more experienced participant "selects, focuses, and feedbacks an environmental experience in such as way as to create appropriate learning sets" (as cited in Palincsar, Brown, & Campione, 1991, p. 77). Feuerstein considered this feature instrumental in providing information about an individual's ability to acquire knowledge; that is, it provides a "*prospective* measure of performance, indicating abilities that are in the process of developing ... [and] is *predictive* of how the child will perform independently in the future" (p. 76). Thus, dynamic assessments provide an indication of what children are capable of learning—their *potential* development—rather than what they have already learned.

We contend that the idea of dynamic assessment is well-suited to investigating conceptual change, with appropriate tailoring to fit the domain-specific context of science. There are two critical variables in conducting successful assessments of this nature: (a) the amount (and kind) of guidance that is provided and (b) the skills and knowledge of the guide with respect to providing assistance in appropriate ways at appropriate times. The first variable concerns the nature of the performance that is expected because the guidance will be a function of the actions required to support the student in culturally appropriate activity. The second variable concerns the issue of forming a ZPD; that is, the ability of the more experienced participant (the guide) to engage the student in a challenging situation and support that student sufficiently to encourage persistence with the task. Thus, the three aspects that need to be addressed in designing a dynamic assessment that is specific to a subject matter domain are: (a) the nature of the task, (b) the activity of the student (includes expected performance), and (c) the activity of the guide. These categories are not mutually exclusive as they are interdependent; however, it is conceptually useful to consider them separately.

The next section describes our conceptualization of the features of dynamic assessment in science (called *dynamic science assessment* [DSA]), specifying the types of opportunities that must be created for the student to engage in actions reflective of the practice of science as well as the role of the guide in mediating that activity.

DSA

A dynamic assessment concerning the domain of science requires a context in which the norms and expectations that guide knowledge production in the scientific community are reflected. A major goal of scientific activity is to develop theories to explain the physical world, and contemporary views of science indicate the prominence of theory in the interpretation as well as explanation of physical phenomena (e.g., Suppe, 1977). Thus, a DSA should engage students in the development of explanations (theories) to account for the critical events or features of particular phenomena that are observed by the student. In addition, scientists create opportunities to test the validity and power of their explanations. This, too, should be a feature of DSA, and such opportunities can be created by the guide or the student.

The nature of the task and materials.   We assume that DSAs will involve students in the observation of actual physical phenomena or simulations of them (e.g., using microcomputer software). Employing an actual phenomenon provides an opportunity for students to test their explanations and receive feedback.[1] We also

---

[1]This feature is in contrast to some methods employed for investigating conceptual understanding that present student participants with representations of the physical world using simple line drawings (e.g., Osborne & Gilbert, 1980).

maintain that it provides a more motivating situation for students, because if they can test out their ideas and adjust them as needed (as do scientists), the adequacy of their initial conceptions is not of concern and they can feel free to bring to bear whatever conceptions are helpful to explain what they observe. The possibility of manipulability of a phenomenon is also important because it emphasizes the active role of the student in that he or she can seek more information about it. For example, in the context of working with electric circuits, although we provided previously constructed circuits for the students to work with, we also provided extra wire that could be used to add new paths to them. We explicitly signaled this support by asking students whether they would like to use the materials to find out more about the circuits.

We recommend that phenomena selected for DSAs involve familiar materials and events, rather than those of an esoteric nature. This makes it more likely that the situation will be accessible to the student participant for engaging in a range of cognitive activities.[2] For example, with respect to assessing students' conceptions of electricity, we constructed simple electrical circuits involving common materials such as batteries, small light bulbs, and thin, insulated wire (the specific circuits are described in the next section). To ensure a challenging situation to foster the construction of a ZPD, discrepant events are particularly useful. In a discrepant event, a result occurs that does not match one's expectation, such as in the case of the equal rate of descent of a heavy and a light object. In the context of electricity, we included circuits in which closing a switch (completing a circuit) functioned to "turn off" light bulbs (by short circuiting them), which provided an unexpected result as that is not how a switch should function in a circuit.

In addition, we recommend that the assessment should include a variety of related phenomena. This allows the guide to examine the extent to which similar ideas are brought to bear in related contexts in which the same conceptions, if consistent with the practice of science, would be expected to be used. It also provides the student with multiple opportunities to use and develop a conception. For example, in our electricity assessment, we used the same basic circuit in three tasks, with each circuit differing only in the number of switches. In each case, the students encountered the same general phenomenon—lighted light bulbs—but whether the bulbs were lighted and to what brightness, differed in the circuits. Thus, students were afforded multiple opportunities to construct explanations for the flow of electricity, to account for the differences in where and how much light was produced in the circuit.

---

[2]That is not to say that esoteric phenomena would not be useful. Indeed, they can be engaging due to their uniqueness and may motivate students to be creative in constructing explanations. As a result, such situations may be revealing with respect to the inventiveness of the child and his or her propensity to change and develop conceptions.

These features help to maximize our potential to observe learning "in action," that is, the response of students to new information that may or may not match their existing ideas. This issue is at the heart of scientific practice because scientists, as well as students, are confronted with the need to reconcile observation and theory. Student responses to a range of phenomena provide insights about the type of information students deem to be helpful in their effort to construct general ideas to explain their observations. These insights are likely to be helpful in understanding conceptual change and indicate how science learning can be promoted through instruction.

The nature of the expected performance and the role of the guide.
Assessments of this nature are conducted in the tradition of a Piagetian clinical interview. As such, one goal of the guide is to ask whatever questions are needed to determine the conceptions of the student participant. To be effective in this goal requires valuing the students' ideas and explicitly signaling that to them by probing their reasons for making particular predictions and explanations, regardless of accuracy. By persisting in getting clarification or elaboration of these ideas until confident of how the ideas make sense to the student participant, the guide also fosters thinking as the student works to identify and communicate his or her ideas.

A typical progression in a DSA task is that students predict what they will observe under specified conditions, provide a reason for their predictions, describe their observations, compare the accuracy of their predictions to their observations and discuss any differences between them, and explain the result, focusing on underlying causes. As a result, regardless of the student's prediction and reason for making it, he or she must try to construct an explanation that accounts for what is actually observed. The demand for explanation across multiple phenomena means that students are expected to go beyond what they observe and construct conceptions about underlying causes.

This progression is similar to the tasks in a method developed by Champagne and colleagues to assess student learning in science, which they call DOE tasks for *describe*, *observe*, and *explain* (e.g., Champagne, Gunstone, & Klopfer, 1985; Champagne, Klopfer, & Anderson, 1980).[3] A DSA differs from this approach principally in that it is a mediated situation, and guidance is provided by the more

---

[3]Having to reconcile observations with explanations may take unexpected turns as reported by Champagne et al. (1985). Following an administration of DOE tasks about the speeds of falling objects of different weights, they observed students who had participated in the assessments conducting their own experiments with the equipment to collect data to support their predictions that objects of different weights would fall at different rates. Several students apparently were not convinced that the observations they made were valid, arguing that "they failed to observe differences in the rates of fall because of the insensitivity of the experimental procedure" (p. 65).

experienced participant. Whereas in a DOE task the interviewer's goal is to prompt the students to describe their already existing ideas, in a DSA task the guide supports the students in going beyond their existing ideas. One way this is fostered is by asking students to discuss the implications of their ideas. Probing for implications allows the guide to check his or her interpretation of an explanation by eliciting further information as well as possibly prompting the students to further develop their conceptions. For example, in our electricity assessments, one student described the flow of electricity in a way that suggested that a pulse of energy moved through the circuit to light the light bulbs. The guide responded by asking how the student accounted for the fact that the light bulbs were lit at the same time because one implication of a "pulse" model of energy is that it would reach each bulb in turn, hence, not providing energy to the bulbs at the same time.

Finally, a major feature of the role of the guide is in mediating student activity. We conceptualize the mediation and guidance in three dimensions: metacognitive mediation, mediation with respect to domain-specific reasoning, and mediation with respect to domain-specific ideas. The first type of mediation is common to any dynamic assessment; in a DSA, we are additionally concerned with the latter forms of mediation.

With respect to domain-specific reasoning, a way to conceptualize this aspect of mediation is the need to reflect the general frame of reference of the community in whose practice the participants are engaged. With respect to science, this refers to the general standards guiding the production of scientific knowledge that we previously described. Thus, constructing a ZPD that allows us to observe conceptual change toward scientific knowledge, we must signal expectations that (a) concepts are consistently applied (when appropriate), (b) different concepts that are employed will be coherent with respect to one another, and (c) a small number of concepts provide a complete description and explanation of aspects of the physical world. Decision making with respect to this facet of mediation is very difficult as the guide must support the students in developing their own ideas as well as encourage them to reconsider them in light of the standards indicated. If this is not done carefully, the assessment may unnecessarily constrain the students' construction of knowledge rather than enabling development along certain paths. We expect that student conceptual development of scientific knowledge will be a function of the extent to which these standards are signaled by the guide, understood and used by the student, and the extent to which the participants can create a ZPD.

With respect to domain-specific ideas, we conceptualize the mediation as focusing students on central concepts in a discipline. For example, in investigating conceptual change in electricity, we asked students to discuss their thinking about the flow of electricity or current. This is an unobservable aspect of an electric circuit, but it is a major conception scientists use to explain circuit behavior. Another example comes from a DSA that we developed about sound (Magnusson, in press; Magnusson & Palincsar, in press). We were interested in upper elementary school students' understandings about the relation between pitch and wavelength, but students typically commented on amplitude rather than wavelength differences.[4] When students did not attend to wavelength differences as well, we prompted them to do so, and when the concept of wavelength was unfamiliar to students, we illustrated it to them and asked them to use it in constructing their explanation.

The latter example illustrates a major difference in this type of assessment, because students were given information (about a way of conceptualizing a phenomenon or about a concept that scientists use to explain a phenomenon) that was not already known to them. An important part of the mediation in a DSA is to provide students with accurate information that is critical to explaining a particular phenomenon, and the guide and student can discuss how that information impacts the student's thinking and conceptions. The key is to know when and how to do this so that it facilitates the development of more elaborated, differentiated, or integrated knowledge. This feature has been presented in some of the research examining science learning, but it has not been considered standard practice in assessing children's learning. For example, in one of Osborne's (1983) studies about children's understandings of simple electric circuits, he included a task in which students where shown (using an ammeter) the amount of current on either side of a light bulb in a circuit. This feature was not part of the assessment approach that Osborne commonly cited in his research, and the description of this study suggested that this task was employed because he was trying to answer the question of how students' understandings can be modified by instruction, not that he considered it part of the assessment of understanding. We consider this difference to be evidence of a common assumption that seems to have guided much of the research of students' understandings: Providing guidance to the student in a way that fostered learning was "out of bounds." In a dynamic assessment, this type of situation is precisely the point of what we are trying to do. In the Osborne study, 32 of 37 students whose initial models of current were scientifically inaccurate changed to a scientifically accurate model of conservation of current when presented with empirical information about the amount of current in different parts of a circuit. This dramatic change provides a contrasting image to the many studies claiming that misconceptions interfere with learning and are resistant to change. As a result, we consider the approach of DSA to be an important addition to our tools for understanding conceptual change in science. We now turn to a discussion of our development of a DSA for use with elementary school students in the topic area of electricity.

---

[4]The DSA involved the use of software that allowed a microcomputer to function as an oscilloscope.

EXAMINING CONCEPTUAL CHANGE IN ELECTRICITY

The Legacy of Previous Studies of Students'
Understanding of Electricity

Tasks for Examining Conceptions of Electricity

Given our context of elementary school students, the basic concepts that we could expect them to use for understanding electricity were current, resistance, and voltage. We examined previous studies to gain information about how these conceptions have been investigated. Most studies of children's conceptions of electricity have focused on understandings of current, and a few have examined conceptions of voltage. Virtually no studies have specifically examined qualitative understandings about resistance, despite its critical role in understanding electricity (e.g., White, 1993). We included tasks relative to each concept in our design of a DSA for electricity; however, for the purposes of this article we focus on the tasks concerning current and resistance.

Current.   The studies that presented students with actual electrical materials and examined students' understandings of current, typically utilized simple electrical materials of batteries,[5] flashlight bulbs, and short lengths of insulated wire, which is consistent with our recommendation of the use of common materials. However, except for one study (Russell, 1980),[6] only series circuits were utilized. We consider this to be a major limitation in previous research because the differences in electrical behavior between series and parallel circuits illustrate central ideas about electricity. In the context in which we were working—we interviewed students following a long-term instructional project during which the students constructed parallel circuits—the students' prior experiences with parallel circuits made it reasonable to include them in our DSA. Moreover, we thought that parallel circuits were necessary to provide sufficient challenge to engage students in ZPDs. We devised our own circuits for examining their ideas of current with respect to parallel circuits.

Resistance.   With respect to resistance, this concept has only been included in investigations of the conceptions of older students (i.e., high school and college). Thus, we developed our own means for investigating this concept, being guided by our knowledge of the students with whom we were working, and the nature of their experiences during instruction in electricity.

---

[5]Dry cells were used, but for convenience they are referred to as batteries.
[6]This study did not include opportunities for participants to observe actual phenomena and check the accuracy of their predictions or to work with the circuit in question.

Frameworks for Representing Conceptions of Electricity

Current.   One strength of some of the previous studies examining students' ideas about current is that they represented those ideas in terms of conceptual or mental models. From the work of Osborne (1983), Russell (1980), and Arnold and Millar (1987), six different models of students' conceptions of current have been identified. These models are depicted in Figure 1. We developed a classification scheme that differentiates these models on the basis of whether current is conceived of as flowing from one or both poles of the battery. Models that indicate that current flows outward both from the negative and positive poles of the battery are referred to as bidirectional conceptions of current because current flows concurrently in two directions. Models that depict a single current are referred to as unidirectional conceptions of current. These classifications allow us to order the models with respect to scientific knowledge because their features indicate particular under-standings about electricity. The unipolar model indicates the least understanding of electricity because it does not include the conception that there must be a complete path for electricity to flow. All of the other models illustrate that conception. The attenuation and sharing models are closest to the scientific model because they indicate a unidirectional rather than bidirectional conception of current, and current is conceived of by scientists as flowing from only one pole of the battery. Thus, the models in the figure are in order from least to most scientific.

Whereas these models are useful in illuminating students' conceptions about series circuits, the extent to which they inform us about students' conceptions of parallel circuits is unknown. We suspect that different models may emerge for two reasons. One is that the perceptual differences between series and parallel circuits may influence student thinking and result in the development of different types of models. The second reason that the models may be different is that the interactive nature of the tasks that we propose to assess student understanding may result in the development of models that have not been previously identified. The validity of this reasoning is an empirical question. Our analysis was designed to answer this question.

Resistance.   We are not aware of any research that has tried to represent students' ideas about resistance. Thus, we devised our own scheme for representing students' conceptions of resistance.

Knowledge of Electric Circuits

Before describing our assessment, a few comments are in order for the reader who may not be knowledgeable about the difference in structure and function between series and parallel circuits or about scientific conceptions of current and

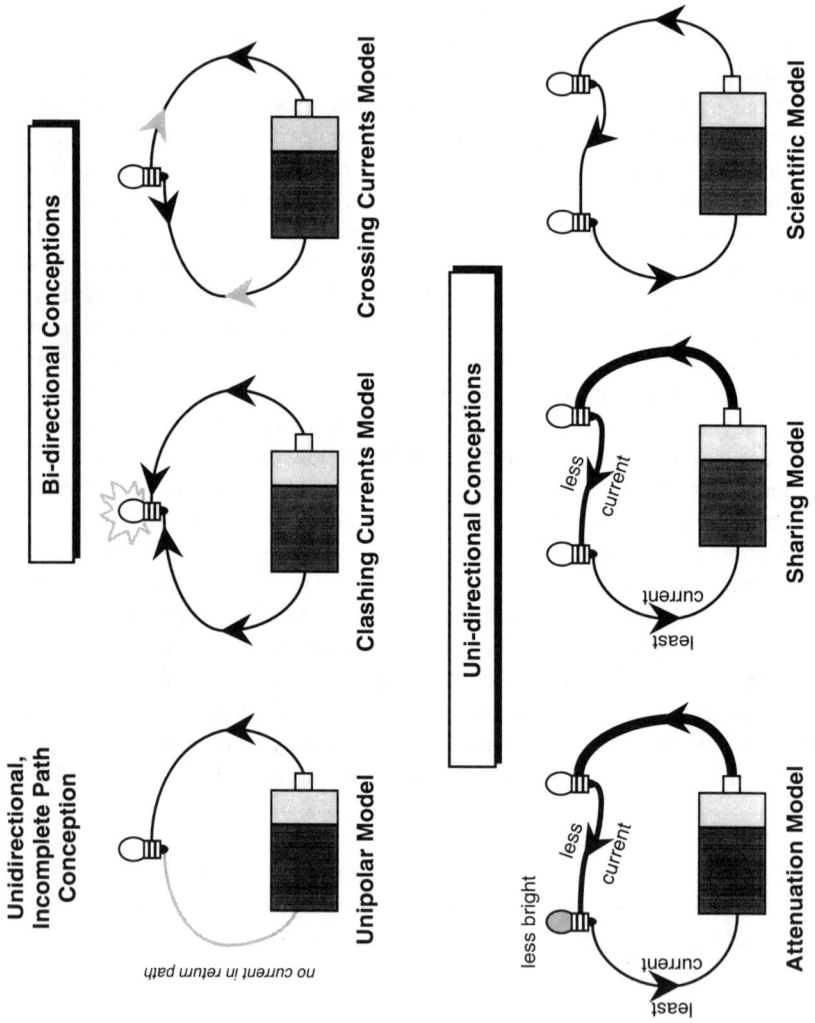

Unidirectional, Incomplete Path Conception

Bi-directional Conceptions

Uni-directional Conceptions

no current in return path

Unipolar Model

Clashing Currents Model

Crossing Currents Model

less current

least current

less bright

less current

least current

Sharing Model

Attenuation Model

Scientific Model

FIGURE 1   Students' models of electric current in simple series circuits. Adapted from Gauld (1988), Osborne (1983), and Shipstone (1985).

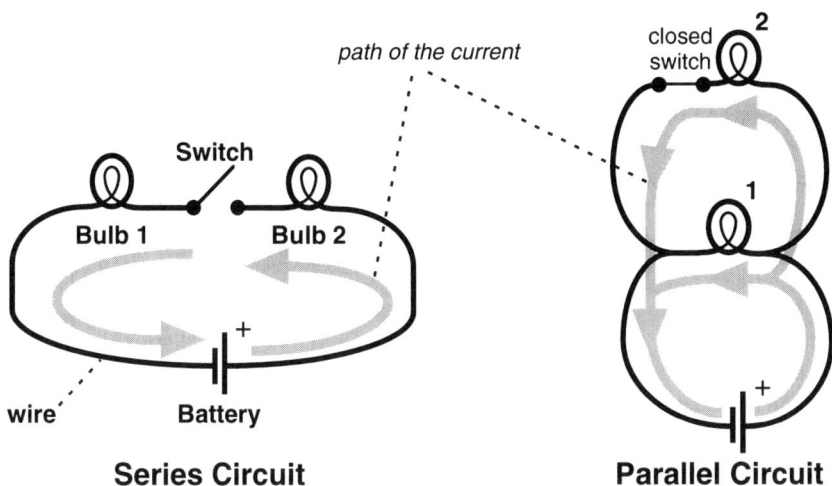

FIGURE 2   Circuit diagrams of the types of simple electrical circuits.

resistance. Figure 2 shows circuit diagrams of an example of each type of circuit. A circuit diagram shows each circuit element in symbolic form, and we have added labels to indicate what element each symbol represents. The plus sign (+) by the battery symbol indicates the location of the positive pole of the battery. This is important information with respect to the direction of the flow of electricity. Switches in a circuit diagram are, by convention, shown in the open position as illustrated by the raised diagonal line in the symbol of a switch. This configuration visually illustrates that when a switch is open there is a lack of connection with the other circuit elements. Thus, an open switch corresponds to what we commonly think of as a switch in the off position. The symbol for a closed switch is also shown in the diagram (the position indicates that the switch is off). The switches that we used look very much like the symbol shown in the figure (they are typically referred to as knife switches), and this provided a visual cue for students that the circuit (or some portion of it) was open or closed.[7]

Current.   Notice that in the series circuit shown in the figure, there is only one possible path for the current to flow. This information is illustrated by arrows showing the path of electricity according to convention in science. With a single path available, any open switches or burned out light bulbs make the circuit

---

[7]Despite our claims that the position of the switch is a positive cue, in pilot work during the development of the DSA for electricity, we encountered a few students (prior to instruction about electricity) who thought that the up position meant that the switch was on because their light switches at home were typically in the up position when the lights were on.

incomplete, meaning that electricity will not flow and no light bulbs will light. In a parallel circuit, there are multiple paths along which electricity can flow (this is also illustrated by arrows in the diagram). As a result, switches on parallel branches of a circuit can be open or light bulbs broken without preventing light bulbs on other branches of the circuit from lighting. For example, if the switch in the parallel circuit shown in Figure 2 were open, Bulb 2 would not light, but Bulb 1 would.

Resistance.   We examined ideas of resistance by constructing circuits in which some wires did not include light bulbs; that is, some paths contained very little resistance. The result was what is commonly referred to as a short circuit; that is, the current takes a path that does not include all the intended circuit elements.[8] In one circuit we accomplished this by taking a separate wire, attaching it to one end of the battery, and touching the other end to different parts of the circuit. Using the series circuit of Figure 2, imagine an additional wire with one end attached to the positive pole of the battery and the other end reaching far enough to touch the left side of Bulb 1. When the switch is closed, both lights in the circuit light, but when the wire added to the battery is touched to the left side of Bulb 1, both lights would go out. The reason for this change is that the additional wire provides another path for electricity to flow, and because there is less resistance in that path, more electricity flows than in the other path with the two light bulbs. The light bulbs do not light because the reduced amount of electricity in the path of which they are a part does not provide enough energy to the light bulbs for their filaments to produce light.

Given these scientific conceptions of current and resistance, we now discuss the specific context of our DSA for electricity.

Designing a DSA for Electricity

Following our specifications for DSAs, we constructed seven circuits for students to explore during our investigation of conceptual change in electricity. For the purpose of this article, we focus on the results for five of those circuits, which were parallel circuits. Decisions about the nature of the circuits that we planned were guided by the principle that they present challenging yet accessible situations for upper elementary school students to discuss. The five parallel circuits that we used in this study are shown in Figure 3. The presence of multiple switches in several circuits provided some manipulability, as did the shorting wire in Circuit 1. We designed Circuit 1, which represents a combination of a series and parallel circuit,

---

[8]The term *short circuit* is misleading because the path does not have to be shorter. Circuit 2 of our assessment circuits is an example of a short circuit in which the path carrying most of the current is, in fact, the longest path in the circuit.

because it provides many different phenomena for students to observe and explain. For example, when both switches are closed, all the lights are lighted, and Bulb 1 is brighter than Bulbs 2 and 3, which are the same brightness. During the DSA, students were expected to explain the brightness differences. In addition, if Switch A is open, only Bulb 1 is lighted, and if Switch B is open (regardless of the position of Switch A), no lights will light. Thus, Switch B is a master switch, and students were expected to explain this feature as well.

It can be seen that a master switch occurs in three out of four of the remaining circuits (the exception is Circuit 2). This is one example of how we have built redundancy into the DSA electricity tasks. By having the same electrical components in different circuits, students encountered the same phenomenon multiple times and were afforded multiple opportunities to construct explanations for them.

We also included a task with Circuit 1 that involved short circuits. The inclusion of this task allowed us to gain insights into students' sense making with respect to the concept of resistance. The shorting task utilized two segments of wire: (a) a 1-ft section that was attached to the positive end of the battery and could be touched to any point on the circuit, and (b) a coil containing approximately 100 ft of wire, from which about 1 ft of wire was uncoiled for similarly easy access to touch any part of the circuit. With these wires, students could make different lights turn off, thereby controlling the lighting in the circuit. For example, when touched to the right side of Bulb 2 (see Figure 3), Bulb 3 will turn off and Bulb 2 will become as bright as Bulb 1. The coil and the short wire, however, produced different results because of the difference in length.

The remaining circuits that were used in our assessment are variations of student-generated circuits that were created by students during their instructional project. Circuits 2 and 3 are representations of circuits used by students in a class that had the task of lighting stores in a scale model of a shopping mall that they designed and built. The stores were narrow ($\approx$16 in.) but long ($\approx$3 ft), and several student groups decided to place several lights on one long circuit along the wall of their model stores. These lights did not need to be independently controlled, because it is common for all the lights in a store to be turned on at once; hence the students reasonably chose to use a single switch. On the other hand, the different location of the switch in Circuits 2 and 3 makes a tremendous difference in its effect. In Circuit 2, the lights go off when the switch is closed, which is contrary to common wiring practices. This happens because the switch in Circuit 2 acts to "short" the circuit because it provides a path with less resistance than the other paths, causing the majority of electricity to flow through it and leaving too little electricity to light the bulbs on the other paths. Clearly, this is not a desirable configuration for a circuit in a real building; however, it accomplished what the students needed it to do which was to turn off the lights. In contrast, in Circuit 3 the lights are off when the switch is open. Circuit 4 is a combination of elements in Circuits 2 and 3, which is another example of how we built redundancy into the DSA.

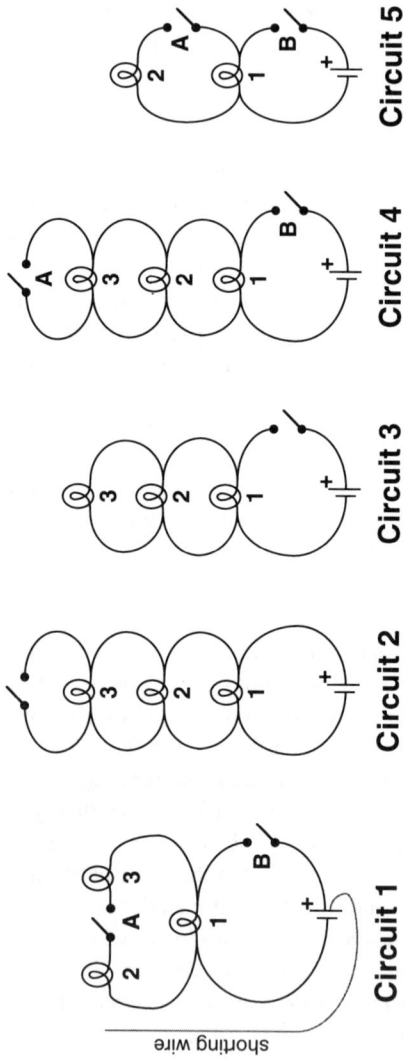

FIGURE 3   Diagrams of circuits employed in a dynamic science assessment students' understanding of electricity.

Circuit 5, although similar in features to the other circuits, was included to give students the opportunity to rewire the switches in a circuit to achieve a different effect. As configured in the diagram, Switch B must be closed in order for Switch A to be functional in turning Bulb 2 on and off. Students were asked how they could rewire Circuit 5 so that they could independently turn off each light with a switch. We could have used Circuit 4 for this task, but that would have been a more complex task than was desired because it involved rewiring circuits for three light bulbs.

Research Questions

With this collection of circuits, we thought that we had a sufficiently challenging situation so that students would find the need to develop their existing conceptions or construct new ones, and a sufficient amount of redundancy to provide multiple opportunities for them to engage with the guide in a supportive context to facilitate change. Nevertheless, as a new method of assessment, it was important for us to check the validity of this DSA as an assessment of conceptual change in electricity. Two questions guided us in investigating the validity of this assessment:

- What evidence was there that the assessment provided opportunities to place students in ZPDs about electricity?
- In instances of ZPDs, did the assessment discriminate students according to their potential to develop scientific knowledge?

After searching for evidence confirming or disconfirming the validity of this assessment for its intended purpose, our culminating research question concerned information about conceptual change in electricity. We asked:

- What picture of conceptual change in electricity emerged from these assessment results?

RESEARCH DESIGN

The research reported in this article was conducted as part of a larger effort to make science instruction at the elementary school level more authentic and meaningful. This effort involved five classes spanning the second through fifth grades. The science instruction was framed by the question: How can we light a (space or building)? The students, working in small groups, were responsible for planning and constructing a scale model of the designated space (e.g., a zoo) or building (e.g., a house, a mall) as well as planning and building electric circuits to light it (Magnusson, Karr, George, & Boyle, 1994). Minimum numbers of lights were required (appropriate to the structure), and students were expected to wire them so that they could be operated independently; that is, a light switch in a room was expected to turn on one or just a few lights (as is the case in a typical room in a house) not every light in the structure. This requirement meant that the students had to build parallel circuits to have the lights lighting independently, and to have the lights sufficiently bright if they chose to have multiple lights on one circuit.

Participants

The school involved in the electricity instruction was located in a small midwestern town near a large city. The school draws from a lower middle-class community, which contains subsidized housing, and has a relatively large percentage of African Americans. Participants in the research included students in third- through fifth-grade classes. Students from these classes were selected in consultation with their teachers so that the range of students in each classroom, with respect to socioeconomic status, gender, ability, and ethnicity, was represented. Approximately one fourth of the students in each class participated in the assessment, for a total of 28 students.

Conducting the Assessment

Circuits were initially presented to the students with wires disconnected from the batteries and with all switches closed. Students were shown one circuit at a time, and in keeping with the features of DSA assessment tasks, students were asked to predict what they would they see when the wires were connected to the batteries, and to provide a justification for their predictions. Following that, they observed what actually happened in the circuit and, regardless of the accuracy of their prediction, were prompted to explain why they thought the phenomenon that they observed had occurred. Students were allowed to further work with and make minor changes in the circuit to gain additional information about the circuit if they chose to do so. During this type of activity, the guide prompted students to explain how what they were doing helped to inform their thinking, as well as what the results of their action with the circuit indicated to them. Occasionally, students were asked what they could do to the circuit to test their explanation.[9]

Assessment conversations were conducted at the end of the school year in which students participated in the electricity project. The bulk of students' experiences with electrical materials had taken place earlier in the school year (roughly

---

[9]A copy of the complete protocol is available from Shirley J. Magnusson on request.

November–February), but additional activity occurred a few weeks before the interviews as students prepared for a "lighting" ceremony—a public exhibition of the models for parents and other community members important to the school. During formal instruction, students did conduct activities that are typical of instruction about electricity at the elementary school level, and they did have some exposure to the basic concepts of electricity, but the extent and depth of instruction with that focus varied among the teachers.

All of the assessment conversations were led by Mark Templin. He has substantial teaching experience at the kindergarten through Grade 12 level as well as previous experience conducting interviews of a clinical nature. All assessments were conducted at the students' school during the school day. They typically lasted from 45 min to 1 hr, and they were audiotaped. Detailed field notes (using circuit diagrams of each circuit) were kept to record information about the students' actions and ideas that would be difficult to discern from an audiotape record.

Documenting Conceptual Change in Electricity

Assessment conversations were transcribed, and those data with their associated field notes formed the corpus of data that we used to understand student learning about electricity. As indicated previously, we were interested in documenting changes in conceptions that occurred during the assessment. We developed the following procedures to accomplish that goal.

Emergent Content Analysis

We call our analytic approach emergent content analysis. We characterize it as a form of content analysis because our intent is to capture the content of what is communicated by the student participants. In addition, because we are interested in their ideas about scientific concepts about electricity, we bring preestablished categories for identifying the type of information in the analysis that will inform us about students' understanding of electricity. For example, the focus of our analysis on students' conceptions of current was informed by our knowledge of previously identified student models for current in series circuits. On the other hand, our approach is different from a content analysis in that we are open to ways of representing the students' ideas that emerge from the data. In the case of documenting students' ideas about current, we developed new models to characterize student conceptions, and those representations emerged from our efforts to construct meaning from the data.

The emergent categories arose from a recursive process of constructing, comparing, and refining specific representations of students' ideas, from circuit to circuit and from interview to interview. They are constructed not only with attention to finding meaningful ways of representing the content of the interview data but also for ease in comparing those ideas to currently accepted scientific knowledge. Thus, the framework guides our meaning making of the student data and is itself modified and embellished by the emergent student themes.[10]

The content focus.   When phenomena are the focus of student assessments, there are always multiple possibilities for the content focus. Whereas a purely interpretive approach might proceed without expectation about the content that could emerge from the data, we acknowledge that our interview protocol was constructed to focus on particular content—students' understandings of current, resistance, and voltage. We see this as a strength because science instruction does have specific content goals, and if we are to facilitate student learning about them then we need to better understand the steps students take in constructing under-standing. Thus, the first-level coding of the data involved marking sections of transcripts in which students discussed their ideas in relation to these central concepts.

Following this coding, we focused on representing the nature of students' ideas about these concepts with respect to each circuit because each circuit included different phenomena and presented different perceptual cues.[11] For the purposes of this article, we focus on the students' conceptions of current, with respect to the direction of flow of electricity, and their conceptions of resistance. Our process in characterizing these data are described in the next section.

Identifying emerging patterns.   Field notes from the assessments suggested that there were patterns in the paths that students traced to indicate how they thought electricity flowed in a circuit. Following the lead of previous studies that described students' conceptions in terms of models of current flow (e.g., Gauld, 1988; Osborne, 1983; Russell, 1980), we similarly sought to identify the models that students' responses suggested. We did not, however, assume that students' ideas from the assessment could be represented by a single model, given the variety of phenomena that students encountered from different circuits. Thus, the analysis of students' ideas was considered separately with respect to each circuit. With respect to resistance, and given our attention to that concept in situations of short circuits,

---

[10]Our concern with regard to comparison with scientific knowledge should not be interpreted as attributing greater status to those ideas. Representations that allow easy comparison with desired scientific knowledge simply permit us to more readily identify the aspects of students' thinking that are consistent with scientific knowledge.

[11]By perceptual cues, we mean that there are features of the physical layout of a circuit that may suggest explanatory ideas to an observer.

we were guided by our own knowledge of electricity to focus on whether and in what amount students conceptualized that current was flowing in the wire that comprised a short circuit. In the next section, we present our findings with respect to students' conceptions of current and resistance.

RESULTS

Validity Evidence for Our DSA in Electricity

Our first research question concerned whether our DSA about electricity was valid with respect to creating opportunities and supporting change in students' conceptions. The determinant for that validity issue was having evidence that the assessment engaged students within ZPDs and changed with respect to accepted scientific knowledge. Recalling that a ZPD is a cognitive space created by the interaction of the interviewer and the student in which new understandings can develop, assessing whether this occurred involved examining the interview data and documenting instances where opportunities for change existed and occurred.

Forming a ZPD and Supporting Changing Conceptions of Electricity

Our examination of the assessment data indicated that for all but one student, Greg,[12] there were multiple opportunities for developing new understandings, either with respect to current flow or electrical resistance or both. Greg exhibited accurate knowledge with respect to electricity at the outset of the assessment, and we were not able to place him in sufficiently challenging situations in relation to his initial knowledge to create a need for change. We saw little evidence in his interview that a ZPD formed around these circuit problems because he was able to explain circuit problems with virtually no guidance by the interviewer. Thus, our data provided information about Greg's actual rather than his potential development.

We found that all other students in our sample had multiple opportunities to enter ZPDs on a range of issues related to current flow and electrical resistance in the course of their assessments. These opportunities led to three different outcomes that we have categorized as follows: (a) student-missed ZPD opportunity, (b) guide-missed ZPD opportunity, and (c) student and guide in a ZPD. There were few interactions in which the student missed opportunities to engage in a ZPD with the guide, and some interactions in which the guide missed opportunities to engage the student in a ZPD. The data primarily revealed that the vast majority of interactions reflected engagement within ZPDs that afforded opportunities for

---

[12]All student names are pseudonyms.

students to develop scientific knowledge. The result of these opportunities was that during the assessment conversations all but two students exhibited changing conceptions with respect to electric current or resistance.

In the three subsections that follow we describe each of these outcomes, and we provide vignettes illustrating the most critical outcomes with respect to this type of assessment: the guide missing a ZPD opportunity and the student and guide engaged within a ZPD. Each vignette is illustrative of a typical interaction for the particular category of opportunity outcome.

Student-missed ZPD opportunity.   At times, students missed opportunities to enter ZPDs with the guide. This typically occurred when the student and guide did not share one or more fundamental notions of electricity. In one instance, when dealing with the behavior of Circuit 1 in the case of a short at Bulb 2, the student observed that Bulbs 1 and 3 lit. The guide—hoping to provide a point of entry into a zone by beginning on common ground—asked, "Is there electricity going through the circuit right now?" The student replied, "No," and the guide responded by prompting the student to reexamine this impossibility by asking, "So the bulbs are lighting up without any electricity?" The student's response, "Yeah. They are." was again questioned by the guide. When the student did not respond and gave no indication he would reconsider his conception, the guide moved on to a different issue.

This dialogue could be interpreted as an act of a nonresponsive student; however, the student and guide continued their discussion for 30 more minutes without further incident of this kind and throughout the assessment the student remained pleasant and amiable. Hence, it seems that the conversation, for whatever reason, went momentarily beyond this student's zone of proximal development. As such, the dialogue was truncated by the lack of coherence between the empirical evidence, the guide's response expectations, and the student's conception.

Guide-missed ZPD opportunity.   In addition to occasions in which students missed opportunities to engage in a ZPD with the guide, there were several instances in which the guide missed an opportunity to engage a student in a ZPD. For example, early in Janice's assessment, she described a bidirectional bouncing flow of electricity through Circuit 2. The guide accepted this response by summarizing the essence of her flow model and asking for elaboration. Because the type of model Janice described does not have electricity flowing through the bulbs, the guide probed her explanation relative to this weakness. In her response, Janice began to change her ideas about the flow of electricity, this time describing a partially serpentine unidirectional model.

Okay. How does it make the bulb light? [long pause] Oh! [long pause] O...K. [long pause] Goes from [the battery] then it goes through this [wire] to the bulb and comes out here [on the other side of Bulb 1] and then goes to [Bulb 2] and comes back [to the battery] and then through [Bulb 3] and comes back [to the battery].

The guide tried to capture her complex idea in a field note but asked Janice to repeat her response so that he could check the accuracy of his field note. In response, Janice described a different configuration for the current, this time exhibiting a loop model, which she stayed with on further probing. We can only wonder what may have occurred if she had been confronted with the two different ways that she described the return path. There is no certainty that it would have provoked additional observable conceptual change for Janice; however, once this opportunity was missed we do have evidence that the dialogue surrounding this particular problem quickly extinguished itself.

Student and guide in a ZPD.   Our analysis of the interview transcripts revealed that the assessments included a range of electric current and resistance issues that provided opportunities for the student and guide to enter a ZPD. All students in our sample except Greg and two others entered a ZPD either about flow or resistance at least once during their assessment. Hence this outcome represents a common state of affairs for this set of assessment conversations. One such example is shown in Table 1. The table contains an excerpt from dialogue about wires used to short circuit Circuit 1, and we have provided accompanying commentary categorizing the participant's actions to illustrate how they worked within a ZPD. The interview dialogue is represented in terms of turns in the dialogue, which we refer to as *moves*. Statements and actions by the guide are italicized to make it easy to differentiate the text. In the commentary, we have bolded the categorical terms to facilitate following the sequence of moves in terms of cognitive activity.

The first aspect of note in the table is the prediction or observation phase, which is standard practice in a DSA. The following phase is explanation, but notice that Cardell is not able to provide an explanation at first (Move 5) or following additional observation and a conceptual cue (Moves 6–8). We know that the result is surprising to Cardell, and it is not unexpected that he could not provide an explanation at first, just as it is difficult for scientists to reconcile their conceptions or theories in the face of unexpected results. Finally, following a second cue (Move 9), Cardell ventured a possible explanation (Move 10).

We argue that these conceptual cues were critical to the formation of a ZPD, which we can see in that Cardell did not simply parrot back the cues, but moved beyond them by bringing into the dialogue his own ideas about a relation between energy from the battery and the thickness of the different shorting wires. The next segment of the dialogue (Moves 11–20) revealed these ideas as a result of mediation by the guide to support Cardell in elaborating and extending his ideas, including making a suggestion about what Cardell may mean.

TABLE 1
Assessment Dialogue Excerpt Illustrating Working Within a ZPD for
Developing Scientific Knowledge of Electricity

Move	Participants' Statements[a]	Commentary[b]
1	*What do you think will happen if I touch it [the spool of the red wire] over here to Bulb 3?*	**Request** *for prediction.*
2	About the same thing [as what happened when the red wire was touched to Bulb 2], except [Bulb 3] will cut off and them two [Bulbs 1 and 2] will stay on.	**Prediction** constructed using information from previous observation of Bulb 2 being touched.
3	*[G touches red wire to Bulb 3. All bulbs dim.]*	*Shows phenomenon.*
4	They all stay on.	**Observation**
5	*Why do you think it gets dim? [pause] Why do you think it doesn't go completely out?*	*Request for explanation.* **No response** from Cardell.
6	*I think if you touch the white wire there, it'll go completely out. [Cardell tries it.] [G repeats shorting with red spool of wire.] But this one only gets dim.*	*Suggestion to make an additional observation.* **Cue** *to compare the results for each wire.*
7	*Any idea why that is?*	*Request for explanation.*
8	No	
9	*Do you think it might have something to do with the wire?*	**Cue** *to focus on the nature of the shorting wire.*
10	Maybe it's too many.	**Explanation.**
11	*What do you mean?*	*Request for elaboration.*
12	Like it's going in all the wires, and it's taking up all the battery's energy and it's making it dimmer.	**Elaboration** involving the battery's energy and the circuit's response.
13	*Why do you think the red wire would do that?*	*Request for further explanation.*
14	Well, 'cause I think [the red wire's] thinner and [the white wire] is thicker.	**Extension of explanation.**
15	*Oh. Why do you think that would make a difference?*	*Request for additional extension of explanation.*
16	It takes more energy?	**Tentative additional extension.**
17	*The red wire would or the white wire would?*	*Request for clarification.*
18	The white wire.	**Clarification.**
19	*Would it take more energy from the battery?*	*Suggests elaboration of Cardell's conception.*
20	I think.	**Tentative confirmation** of elaboration.
21	*Now when it takes that energy. …What do you mean by "takes more energy."*	*Request for elaboration of earlier statement.*
22	'Cause it's more wire than it's supposed to be, and it's coming from—I think this is not coming over there. See? [He shorts the circuit with the white wire and uses hand gestures to show where the energy is moving.]	**Manipulation** of circuit to check and illustrate conception.
23	*Uh-huh.*	

(Continued)

TABLE 1 (*Continued*)

Move	Participant's Statements[a]	Commentary[b]
24	It goes up.	Continued illustration of conception.
25	*When you say "takes more energy," do you mean the white wire takes more energy away from the circuit?*	**More specific restatement** of conception.
26	Yeah. See like. [Cardell again demonstrates.]	**Confirmation** and illustration of restatement.
27	*Why do you think that the red wire isn't able to take as much electricity away?*	**Request** for extension of explanation. ["Electricity" mistakenly substituted for "energy."]
28	Because it's thinner.	**Explanation.**
29	*Oh, I see. OK. Well, let's look at the next circuit.*	**Affirms** and **ends dialogue** on this problem.

Note. ZPD = zone of proximal development.
[a]Guide's statements are italicized. [b]Guide's actions are italicized.

The last segment of the dialogue excerpt shows the guide returning to a statement made by Cardell to check his understanding of Cardell's conception. The return resulted in Cardell engaging in additional manipulation of the circuit, presumably to illustrate his ideas to the guide, but it may also have functioned to solidify his own thinking. It is not uncommon in such instances for students to add to or change their conceptions. In a more traditional assessment, we would not have seen any of this development of ideas because the conversation would not likely have progressed past Move 5. Had that been the case, we would have erroneously concluded that Cardell had limited ideas concerning the short circuits. Instead, Cardell indicated possible understanding of several important ideas about electricity: that electricity flows even though the circuit is shorted and no lights are lit, and the thickness of a wire influenced the flow of energy through it.

Looking at this segment as a whole, we see a complex interplay between the student and the guide, with each shifting their participation as the dialogue progressed. For example, we see the manipulation of the circuit pass from the guide's hands—as a tool for asking questions—to the student's hands, as a tool which helped him demonstrate his understanding and clarify his meaning to the guide. On the conceptual side, we also see the development of Cardell's idea from no stated conception (Move 8), through a tentative conception (Moves 10, 16, and 20), to a conception with which the student was finally confident (Moves 26–28). As such, we view this dialogue as an example of conceptual change within a context which allowed shifts in participation to take place. In this case, the mediation was quite conservative, and the change occurred within an ontological category that does not pose great cognitive change, in our thinking. Nevertheless, many students assumed that electricity cannot be flowing if there is not an observable result that it is, such as lighted bulbs, so it is important to recognize the more advanced thinking of Cardell over those students. This idea is developed more fully in the next section.

Discriminating Students With Respect to Developing Scientific Knowledge

Having established that the assessments functioned as intended to illuminate the ideas that students developed with assistance, we turn to our results concerning what the assessments revealed about students' conceptions of electricity. We present our results separately for current and resistance.

Students' models of the path of current in parallel circuits.   Analysis of the data indicated that a small number of models could account for the range of student conceptions exhibited during the assessments. A complete discussion of the models is beyond the scope of this article; however, a few comments are necessary to describe differences in them with respect to the accuracy of knowledge of electric circuits that they imply. Figure 4 shows the models that we identified. We have organized them first according to whether current is viewed as bidirectional, meaning that it is pictured as flowing out from both poles of the battery, or whether it is unidirectional, meaning that current is pictured as flowing out of only one end. Second, we placed the models in order in the figure ranging from the type representing the least scientific conceptions (at the left) to those indicating the most scientific conceptions (at the right). We turn now to the discussion of these types.

The bouncing models suggest to us that students have literally superimposed a model of flow for a series circuit onto the physical configuration of a parallel circuit. Students using this model type have partially scientific knowledge of electricity because the model indicates there must be a complete path for electricity to flow. On the other hand, the bouncing behavior indicated by the model gives the conception a lack of specificity regarding current at the light bulbs. If the current "bounces" up one side of the circuit and down the other side, then it does not necessarily pass through the light bulbs; thus, as a model, it leaves ambiguous the role of current in lighting a bulb.

The loop model, which we only observed with students employing unidirectional flow models, is a slightly more advanced conception from the bouncing model because, in addition to signaling the need for a complete path, it indicates that electricity must pass through the light bulbs in order for them to light. In this model, students traced the flow of electricity in such a way as to first pass through all of the circuit elements and then somehow return directly to the battery. The limitation of this model was that tracing a single loop through a parallel circuit meant that students were forced to skip over or retrace wires in the circuit, which is not scientifically accurate.

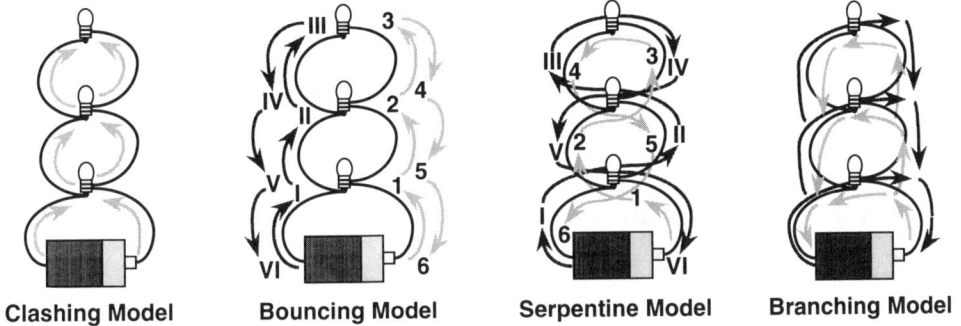

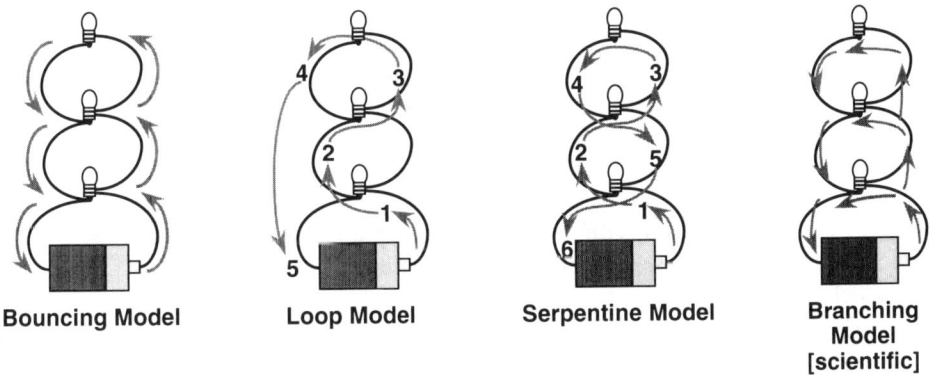

FIGURE 4   Students' models of the path of electric current in parallel circuits.

The serpentine model is a particularly interesting conception because it appears to us also to be a case of students imposing a conception of the flow of electricity in a series circuit to that of a parallel circuit. With this model, imagine tracing the circuit in a figure-8 fashion with a string, and then "untwisting" it; it becomes a single path or a loop. Unlike the loop model, however, it flows through all the circuit elements in a nonredundant path, and unlike the bouncing model, electricity clearly flows through the bulbs. Thus, it indicates a more advanced conception of electricity than either of those models. It is an intriguing model with respect to interpreting students' understanding because they are clearly not being cued by the physical appearance of the circuit. At the same time, it is not scientifically accurate because it cannot explain the fact that unscrewing one of the light bulbs in the circuit does not result in the other light bulbs going out, as would be the case if the current flowed along the single path indicated in the serpentine model.

Finally, the most advanced models with respect to developing scientific knowledge of the flow of current are the branching models. The unidirectional version of the branching model is scientifically accurate, although it is not a complete conception with respect to current because it does not indicate anything about the relative amount of current in each branch. Nevertheless, we consider branching models to represent a substantial conceptual leap over the other models because they indicate that electricity simultaneously flows along multiple paths. This difference may be indicative that a shift in ontological category is required because if electricity is thought of as a material substance rather than a form of energy (e.g., Reiner, Chi, & Resnick, 1988), it is more difficult to conceive of it as branching.

Changes in students' models.   One type of change that occurred during the assessments was across model class; that is, some students changed from a unidirectional model to a bidirectional model and vice versa. Although we did not make much of a distinction between bi- and unidirectional models in our differentiation of the models in Figure 4 on the basis of scientific accuracy, we consider change across model class to be non-trivial. Our analysis suggested that there was a pattern of difference by grade level because a substantially larger percentage of third graders than fifth graders employed both bi- and unidirectional flow models during their assessment (44% vs. 23%). Our sample size was not sufficient to statistically test the significance of this difference, but we note it because it may be evidence of a developmental progression away from utilizing conceptually conflicting models.

The other major result concerning students' conceptions of current flow was that many students changed types of models, and that the changes included moves to more and moves to less advanced models with respect to a scientific conception of current. To represent this finding, we categorized all of the students according to whether their models changed with respect to a branching model of current flow. The students who changed conceptions were divided into groups on the basis of whether the change in their model was only momentary; that is, they employed a different model at some point during the interview but returned to their initial conception, or whether they changed and maintained a new model. This classification resulted in six groups of students, and the results by grade level are shown in Figure 5.[13]

---

[13]As indicated previously, the sample configuration did not allow us to empirically examine whether grade level differences were meaningful; nevertheless, we report the results by grade level because we thought the differences were interesting and may be significant. We hope these results encourage others to examine developmental differences in domain-specific conceptual development.

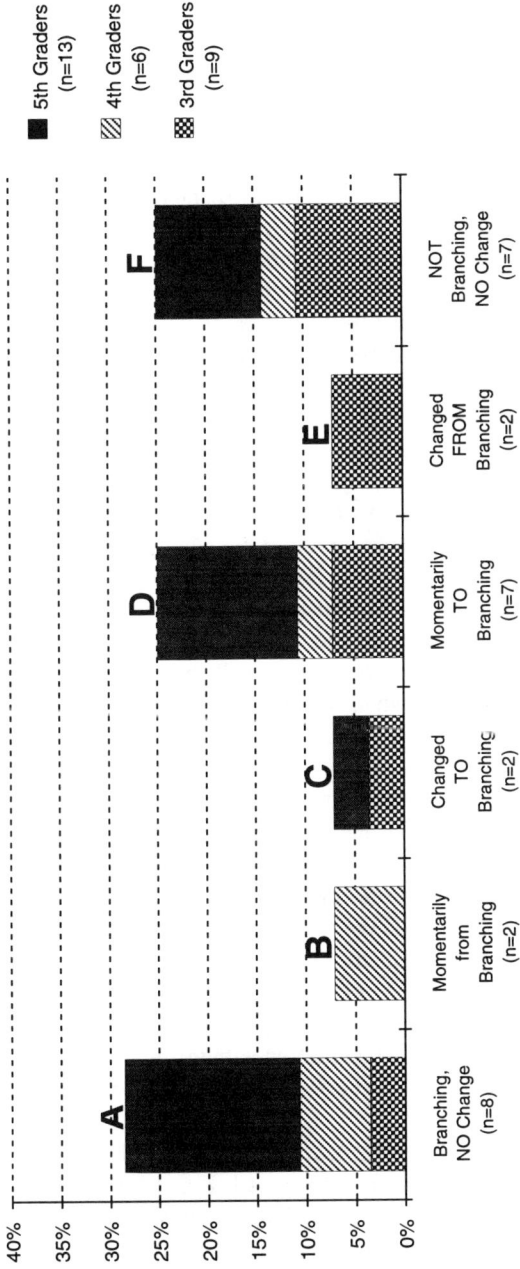

Conceptions of Electric Current

FIGURE 5   Outcomes regarding change toward an accurate model of current flow.

This figure shows the categories in order by accuracy of knowledge and the potential to develop scientific knowledge. The first three groups of students (from left to right) ended the assessment using a branching model. Students in Categories A and B appeared at the outset of the assessment to have accurate knowledge, and even though students in Category B were not able to maintain their conception under some circumstances, we consider them to have great potential to develop a more robust branching conception. Students in Category C are interesting because they developed a branching model during the assessment. In a traditional assessment, these students would have been categorized as having nonbranching conceptions. The fact that they developed and maintained a branching model during the assessment, in the face of increasingly more difficult circuits, suggests that they developed robust knowledge or that they have strong potential to do so.

Students in Categories D, E, and F ended the interview employing a nonbranching model. This result for the students in Category E was intriguing because they began with a branching model and we would predict that the greater explanatory power of that conception would favor it over others. One explanation for the change is that it indicated that the students' initial conception was weak and it collapsed under the challenge of more complex circuits. We would say that these students have the potential to develop a robust branching conception because we know they can conceptualize branching; however, they may have a more difficult time than students in Category D. Students in Category D are interesting because they developed a branching conception during the assessment, and their placement in this category means that this development typically occurred in response to more complex circuit problems. Although these students did not end the assessment with a branching model, we view them as having potential to develop a branching model, and we think that they have greater potential than those students in Category E because they developed the conception under challenging conditions.

These results indicate to us that the assessment was functioning to challenge students and support them in changing toward more accurate models. Moreover, they indicate that the assessment discriminated students with respect to the stability and accuracy of their conceptions. We find it noteworthy that almost half of the students in the sample exhibited a change in model, and that of those, 39% showed the potential to develop knowledge of branching current in a parallel circuit. On a traditional assessment, it is likely that many of these students would have been identified as having conceptions that interfered with the development of scientific knowledge. The results of this DSA suggest quite a different picture.

Students' conceptions of resistance.   Students' ideas about resistance were examined by drawing on data from Circuits 1, 2, and 4. In Circuit 1, the tasks with the shorting wire provided information about students' conceptions; in Circuits 2 and 4 (see Figure 3), the switch wired in parallel at the top of the circuit shorted the circuit when closed, causing two of the three light bulbs to go out (the bulb closest to the battery was slightly lit), and that resulted in a challenging problem for students to explain as well as provided information related to their conceptions of resistance. Figure 6 shows the decision-making schemes that we developed for rating students' knowledge about resistance from the data concerning these circuits. We did not consider any of the students' conceptions to be complete scientific conceptions of resistance, but we did characterize some students as having some scientific knowledge of resistance (designated as "accurate" in the figure).

Circuit 1: In Circuit 1, the starting point for assessing students' understanding concerned whether they thought electricity flowed through the shorting wire (see Figure 6a). When the shorting wire was added to the circuit and students observed changes in the number and/or brightness of lighted bulbs, we evaluated their responses with respect to whether they thought that electricity was flowing through the wire. Students who did not think electricity flowed through the shorting wire were rated as having nonscientific knowledge. One example of a student statement indicating that conception is the following: "There's not energy going through this [white wire]. The white wire is acting like a switch and stopping that from working."

With the students who thought electricity was flowing through the shorting wire, we examined whether they thought electricity was flowing through the shorting wire instead of other circuit elements, and whether they had any ideas about the amount of electricity flowing through the shorting wire. Some students thought that the electricity in the shorting wire somehow prevented electricity from flowing to the bulbs or acted to stop the flow to the bulbs. This conception is indicated in the next excerpt, with the guide's statements in italics.

Why did the bulb go out? 'Cause [the white wire] is blocking it. *The white wire is blocking it?* Yeah. *How is it blocking it? ... Show me how the electricity is going right now?* From [the battery] all the way around [to the end of the white wire]. *Once it gets [to the end of the white wire], then where does the electricity go?* Nowhere else I guess. *So it just goes to the end of the white wire and stops?* Uh-huh. *The electricity goes to here and then stops? Like that?* Yeah, 'cause it doesn't have one of these wires to come back to that [the negative pole of the battery] and make it light up from the positive side. *Okay. It doesn't have a wire that comes back.*

Students exhibiting this type of conception were also judged as having nonscientific knowledge with respect to the concept of resistance.

Other students thought the wire allowed electricity to flow so that it bypassed the bulbs. This conception is shown in the following excerpt.

[Bulb 3] is getting a lot more energy. *How?* Skipping that one I guess. *How is Bulb 2 getting skipped?* It made it go off. *Yeah, but how is that happening? Any idea? Hmm. ... Any idea why that is happening?* Not really.

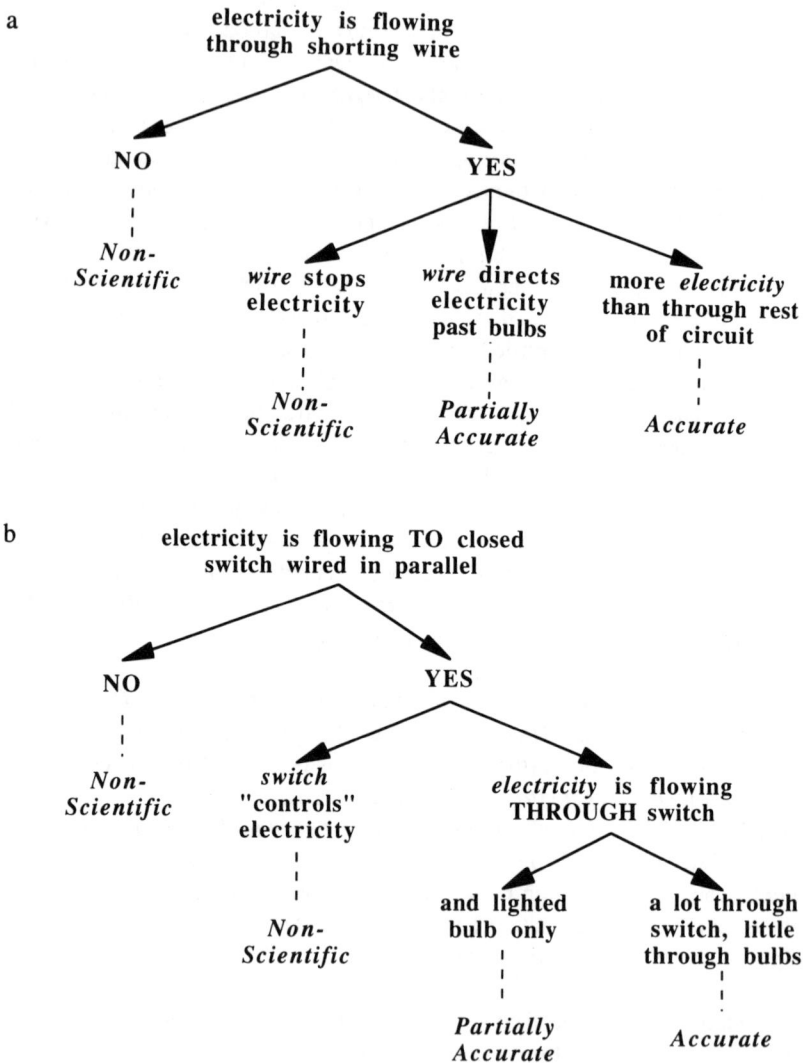

FIGURE 6 Schemes for rating students' conceptions about resistance from their explanations of short circuits.

We judged this conception to contain partially accurate knowledge regarding resistance because it suggests that electricity does not always flow along available paths; however, this conception falls short of understanding resistance as the reason for preferential flow.

Finally, there were students who indicated that much more electricity flowed through the shorting wire than in the rest of the circuit. We judged this conception to represent accurate knowledge with respect to resistance because it correctly characterized the differences in the amount of current in parts of the circuit. The following statement by one student illustrates this conception. "The white wire is taking most of it away. ... Usually you could tell if there's electricity going through it 'cause it gets hot." Although this conception does not represent a complete scientific conception of resistance because the student has not explained why more electricity would flow through a part of the circuit, or how one would know whether it would; nevertheless, we think that having the understanding of differential flow situates the student for developing more complete scientific knowledge of resistance.

Circuits 2 and 4: As we explained earlier, the switch wired in parallel created a short circuit in these circuits when the switch was closed, and we consider explaining this short circuit to be more difficult than in Circuit 1 because the switch appears to operate in a contradictory manner to what students observed during their investigations in the instructional unit. When the switch is open in these circuits, the lights are on, and when the switch is closed, the lights go off, with the exception of the light closest to the battery. As you may imagine, the students found this phenomenon puzzling, and they varied in the extent to which they were able to successfully explain what occurred.

In these circuits, the starting point for assessing students' understanding concerned whether they thought electricity flowed through the switch wired in parallel. Figure 6b shows our scheme for rating students' understandings with respect to resistance in these circuits. If students did not think any energy flowed to the closed switch they were rated as having nonscientific knowledge. This conception is indicated in the following excerpt.

[Electricity is] probably not going through there, 'cause if electricity was going through there it would go on to the light bulbs, 'cause it can't just go like this—straight up. *So in order to get up to that switch, the electricity has to go through those light bulbs?* Uh-huh. Because, see, it has to go through here [the wires in the parallel branches leading to the switch] to light bulbs.

Similarly, if students thought electricity was flowing to the closed switch, giving it an active role, but did not think electricity flowed through the switch, they were assessed as having nonscientific knowledge. One student's statements indicating this conception is shown.

[Circuit 4] When the switch is closed, it doesn't let any more electricity go back. It doesn't let the electricity go back the same way. *So when the switch is open ... the electricity is going up to it and then coming back?* Yeah. *And then when the switch is closed?* It don't let it go back, it just stops.

Finally, students who thought electricity was flowing through the switch were assessed with respect to whether they thought electricity was flowing throughout the circuit or just through the switch and the lighted bulb. If they thought that electricity was flowing through the circuit and the lighted bulb only, they were assessed as having partially accurate knowledge with respect to resistance. The following excerpt from a discussion in Circuit 2 illustrates this conception.

The way the switch is set up it's shorting the circuit. *Do you think there is a little bit or a lot of electricity going through that closed switch right now?* Yeah, there's a little bit.

If they thought that electricity was flowing throughout the circuit, but mostly through the switch, then they were rated as having accurate knowledge with respect to resistance. The following excerpt from a discussion of the behavior in Circuit 4 illustrates this conception.

The electricity is going from [the battery] to [the switch at top] and stuff. And then it's taking a lot of energy going from here [one pole of the battery] and back to here [the other pole of the battery]. *So there's a lot of energy going up to the switch?* Yeah, it's using a lot of energy.

Changes in students' conceptions of resistance.   Using these schemes to track students' conceptions related to resistance, we classified students into groups based on whether their conceptions changed toward a more scientific conception of resistance. Figure 7 shows these results, which are presented separately by circuit due to the difference in difficulty of the problems. In this case, there were three possible categories of no change (categories represented by Columns A, C, and F in the figure) because there were three categories of accuracy of knowledge, and as a result there were three possible categories of change (categories represented by Columns B, D, and E).

Circuit 1: The results for this circuit (see Figure 7a) indicate that 38% of the students changed their conception of resistance, and they all moved toward a more scientific conception. This is an important result considering that this change occurred within the exploration of the first circuit. Of the 62% of students who did not change their conception, 25% exhibited accurate knowledge and would not have been expected to change, and 56% exhibited partially accurate knowledge. These results provide evidence that the assessment discriminated students with respect to the stability and accuracy of their conceptions related to resistance, and that it sufficiently challenged a number of students who changed toward more accurate conceptions of resistance, with support.

Circuits 2 and 4:[14] The results across these circuits indicated that the same number of students changed conceptions as for Circuit 1; however, the distribution of the type of change was different (see Figure 7b). The difference in distribution was due to fewer students changing to an accurate conception, and the fact of two students changing to inaccurate conceptions. In the case of those students who did not change their conception, the distribution relative to the accuracy of their ideas was also different from that of Circuit 1. Fewer students exhibited accurate or partially accurate knowledge, and many more students exhibited inaccurate knowledge. These results provide evidence that the assessment discriminated students with respect to the stability and accuracy of their conceptions related to resistance, and they support our contention that the electrical behavior was more difficult for students to explain for these circuits than Circuit 1. Clearly, students were challenged in this situation, and some were provided sufficient support to change their conception to a more scientific one, but we speculate that the lack of change for these circuits may indicate that the guide's mediation was less effective for facilitating change than for Circuit 1.

Potential to develop scientific knowledge: We consider students in Categories B, D, and E to have the potential to develop scientific knowledge of resistance. The students in Category B showed the potential to develop a more scientific conception of resistance, which we would not have known without this type of assessment. Students in Category D showed the potential to develop partially scientifically knowledge, which is an important result because a conception rated as partially accurate indicates a very different conception of the function of the wire causing a short circuit. Again, we note that these students would not have been recognized as being so capable were it not for this type of assessment. Finally, although the students in Category E (a result only for Circuits 2 and 4) changed to nonscientific conceptions of resistance, the fact that they initially exhibited partially accurate knowledge suggests to us that they can develop scientific knowledge. The direction of their change simply tells us that their initial conception was not well-developed, and may also signal that the guide did not employ sufficient mediation to enable them to maintain or extend their initial partially scientific conceptions.

Summary.   In sum, these results provide evidence that the DSA that we developed for electricity was valid with respect to gaining information about

---

[14]These results, although specific to Circuits 2 and 4, should be considered in the context of change across Circuits 2, 3, and 4. Circuit 3 did not include the switch wired in parallel that functioned to short the circuit; nevertheless, students' investigation of this circuit may have been important to changes in their thinking by the time Circuit 4 was discussed.

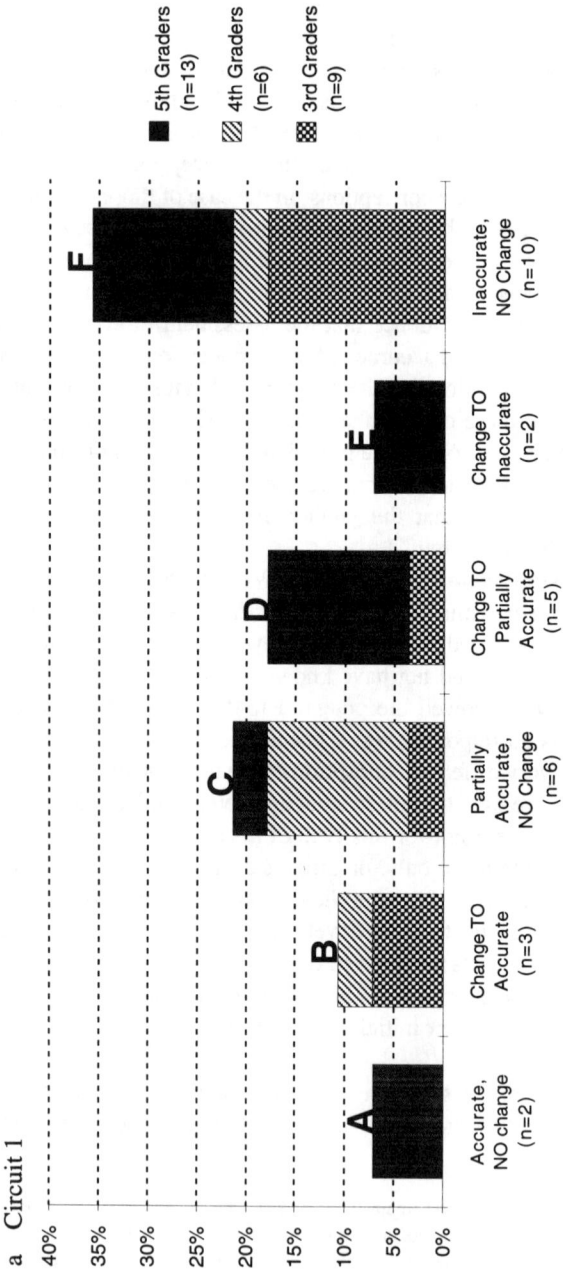

a   Circuit 1

Conceptions of Resistance

Legend:
- 5th Graders (n=13)
- 4th Graders (n=6)
- 3rd Graders (n=9)

Categories:
- A: Accurate, NO change (n=2)
- B: Change TO Accurate (n=3)
- C: Partially Accurate, NO Change (n=6)
- D: Change TO Partially Accurate (n=5)
- E: Change TO Inaccurate (n=2)
- F: Inaccurate, NO Change (n=10)

b Circuits 2 and 4

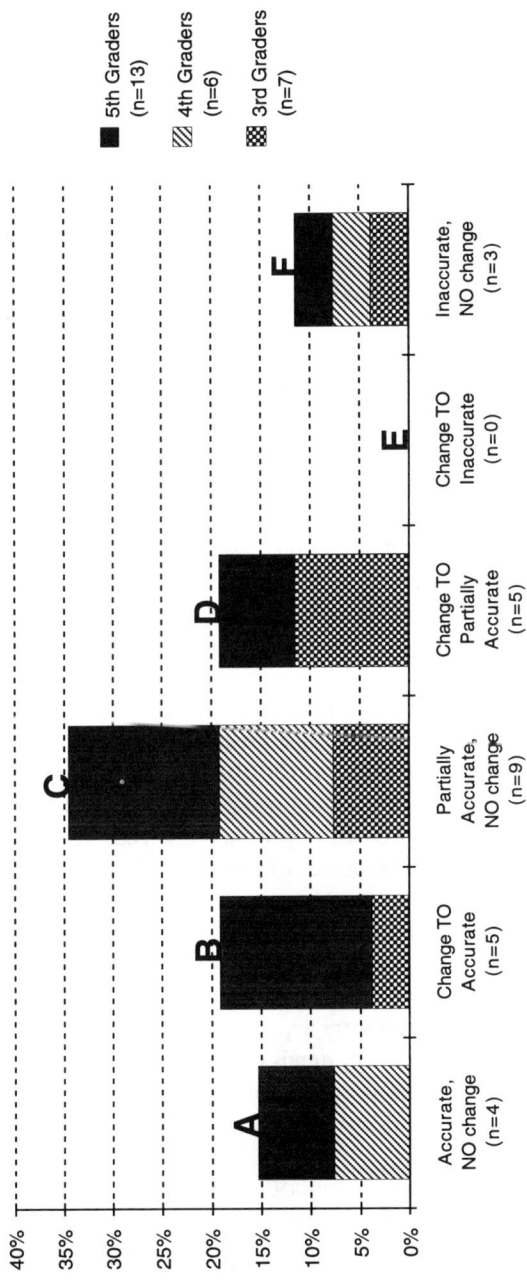

FIGURE 7   Outcomes regarding change in students' conceptions toward an accurate conception of resistance.

133

students' potential for developing scientific knowledge. We were able to represent the changes that occurred in terms of whether particular conceptions were accurate with respect to scientific conceptions of electric current and electrical resistance, and we were able to classify students with respect to their potential to develop robust conceptions matching scientific knowledge. Given these results, we now discuss our findings with respect to the picture of conceptual change in electricity that emerged from our study of these students.

Patterns of Conceptual Change in Electricity

The Interdependence of Conceptions of Current and Resistance

Scientifically, although we can separately define the concepts of current and resistance, they are interrelated when considered in the context of explaining behavior in electrical circuits. For example, in a situation of constant voltage (which is typically the context in instructional activities designed for students of this age) the amount of current in a circuit is inversely proportional to the amount of resistance in the circuit. Furthermore, in the case of multiple available electrical paths in a circuit, current follows the path of least resistance. These relations made it logical to examine students conceptions of resistance with respect to the accuracy of their models of current flow to more fully understand conceptual change in electricity.

To construct this comparison, we examined the data separately for Circuit 1 and Circuits 2 and 4, but we followed the same procedure for categorizing students' conceptions. With respect to conceptions of current, we separated students into two groups: those who did exhibit a branching model by the end of the exploration of a circuit, and those who did not. With respect to resistance, we divided students into three groups according to the accuracy of conception that they exhibited *by the end* of the discussion of the circuit: accurate, partially accurate, and inaccurate. We explored a number of ways to examine patterns in these data, both qualitative and quantitative. Quantitatively, our sample size was too small, given the number of categories that were meaningful, to use statistical analysis without violating the conditions of use for methods that were appropriate to the data. Nevertheless, we think that the results show evidence of trends that we can interpret conceptually in meaningful ways. We present these results graphically in Figure 8, and then discuss their meaning with respect to developing scientific knowledge of electricity.

The importance of a branching model.   Figure 8a shows the results of our analysis of student conceptions of current and resistance with respect to Circuit 1. The relation that is evident here is that no students with a branching model of current exhibited a nonscientific conception of resistance by the end of the exploration of

a   Circuit 1

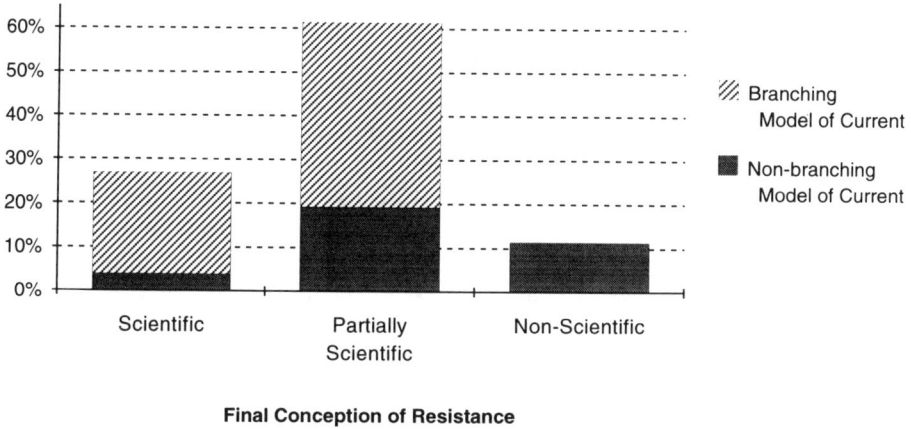

Final Conception of Resistance

b   Circuits 2 and 4

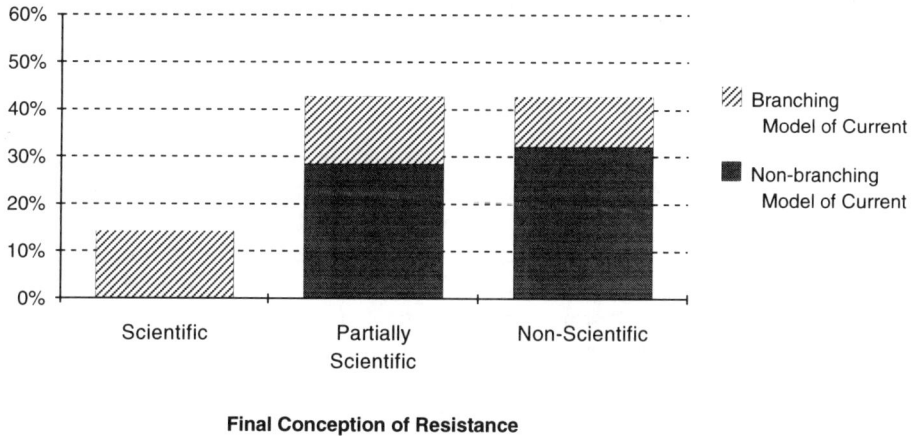

Final Conception of Resistance

FIGURE 8   Relation between scientific knowledge of electric current and resistance.

this circuit. Thus, having a conception that current can branch seemed to assure that the student conceptualized current as flowing in the shorting wire, which was the minimum requirement for partially accurate knowledge of resistance. If this is true, one way to explain this result is that having a branching model enabled certain views of the circuit, which assisted students in constructing explanations that exhibited some accurate knowledge relative to resistance. The key to exhibiting accurate knowledge of resistance for this circuit was recognizing that there were multiple available paths in which current could preferentially flow. This perspective would be much easier for a student with a branching model to take than a student who conceptualized electricity as only flowing along one path; however, the data indicate that having a branching model did not assure such a perspective. Moreover, there was one student who did not have a branching model who exhibited scientific knowledge of resistance. Our data indicate that this student used a bidirectional model of current for this circuit, which may have enabled him to conceptualize multiple paths for electricity to flow, but for a different reason than if he had a branching model.

Figure 8b shows our results with respect to Circuits 2 and 4, and they also suggest that there is a relation between conceptions of resistance and current. Only students with branching models exhibited scientifically accurate models of resistance; students who did not have a branching model exhibited either nonscientific or partially scientific knowledge. In this case, as with Circuit 1, a branching model seemed to be necessary to scientifically explain the electrical phenomena, but having a branching model did not guarantee that the explanation would be scientific. Thus, a branching model may be necessary for students to accurately explain phenomena involving resistance in electrical circuits, but it is not sufficient to ensure desired development of scientific knowledge.

The Issue of the Nature of an Entity

Another issue that seemed important to us in making sense of conceptual change given these data was consideration of what it meant for students to construct these abstract ideas about current and resistance from the behavior of electricity in concrete materials. With respect to current, we argued that there is evidence of the importance of being able to conceptualize it as branching, yet, we did not address what was required to construct that conception. If we think of electricity as a material substance, as has been suggested is common (Reiner et al., 1988), it seems more difficult to think about it as branching. Why would it do that? How would it be accomplished? regulated? If one is not bound by thinking of electricity as a material, then conceptualizing it as branching can be much less problematic. Perhaps, then, this is a case in which it is useful to think of helping students develop conceptions in a new ontological category: One that does not require electricity to be a material substance. Our data do not speak to the potential of this perspective for conceptual change, but we consider it to be a useful outlook in considering additional mediational tools in future DSAs in electricity.

We see a related issue concerning conceptions of resistance, but in this case involving reconceptualization of a material object: wire in an electrical circuit. Many students were puzzled by the difference in results between the short and long wires used to create short circuits in Circuit 1. Scientifically, explaining the different results requires conceptualizing the wire both as an enabler of electricity and a constraint on its flow. We did not sufficiently explore the short circuit context in Circuit 1 to more extensively describe conceptual change relative to this issue, but we think it bears consideration with respect to learning about electricity.

Taken together, the findings from our DSA paint a more complex picture of the issue of conceptual change in electricity than has been typically portrayed. Most of our participants exhibited a combination of accurate and inaccurate knowledge, and change was not an all-or-nothing proposition. Moreover, although a substantial percentage of the participants exhibited at least partially scientific knowledge at some point during the interview, the robustness of that knowledge varied from individual to individual, and the factors influencing momentary changes toward or away from accurate conceptions could not be determined. Nevertheless, we think these findings are important because they suggest a considerably different picture of conceptual change than has been commonly portrayed in the research literature. Whereas students' misconceptions have been portrayed as resistant to change and interfering with the development of scientific knowledge, we saw students readily change their ideas and change from nonscientific conceptions to scientific ones. Thus, we found these results encouraging with respect to students' potential for conceptual change.

SUMMARY AND CONCLUSIONS

We argued at the outset of this article that criticisms of conclusions about conceptual change pointed to the need to bring different perspectives to bear in understanding conceptual change. One such perspective, a sociocultural view of cognition, has been the basis of our work to reconceptualize domain-specific learning and conceptual change. Working from this different view required developing new tools for investigating and assessing learning and conceptual change. We built on the ideas of developmental psychologists interested in examining change and understanding potential rather than actual development, and developed a new approach to examining learning in science, called dynamic science assessment. The intent of this approach is to foster conceptual change in a mediated learning situation, which we conceptualized as forming a zone of proximal development with respect to activity authentic to the practice of science. DSAs are designed to support students in constructing explanations for behavior they observe from actual physical phenomena, and to change their conceptions so they can be used consistently across problems, fit coherently with respect to other explanations, and form a complete picture with respect to some aspect of the physical world.

Our findings indicated that the elementary school students with whom we worked were able to meet the challenges we set in a DSA involving electrical phenomena, and that previous studies have underestimated the potential for knowledge growth for students of this age. In contrast to Arnold and Millar (1987) and

Russell (1980) who argued that children's erroneous interpretations of series circuits indicated that they were not developmentally ready to understand parallel circuits, our results indicate that students of this age can understand electrical behavior in parallel circuits, at least to some degree. We maintain that the limitations they saw in children's conceptions were a function of the tools that they used. Research in the tradition of their work was an important first step toward understanding conceptual change; however, by focusing only on the knowledge children have already developed and its lack of correspondence with scientific ideas in specific contexts, we were unable to see how rich children's ideas are and what they can do with them. Rather than avoid complexity, we argue that challenging tasks are necessary to help us gain understanding of the issues learners face in developing scientific knowledge.

To learn in challenging situations, however, requires willingness and active participation on the part of the learner, as well as knowledge and skill on the part of the guide to sufficiently reflect the cultural norms and expectations of the community whose knowledge is the standard to which the learner is being guided. In addition, the guide must provide sufficient support to assist students in appropriating the tools of the culture. In this way, the issue of conceptual change, which has been seen as problematic when our everyday knowledge is compared with scientific knowledge, becomes a different issue. It is a matter of learning how to think in a different cultural frame than what we use in our everyday lives. We believe that an important aspect of facilitating this change is to be clear that the desired way of thinking is not intended to replace the child's everyday frame, but to be added to it. To accomplish this, students must be acknowledged for the ideas and perspectives they bring, while at the same time being challenged to develop new ideas and ways of thinking, in the particular context, and they must be helped to be cognizant of the difference in the context so that they also learn when it is important to act within that particular frame. To be sure, this is not easy, and we need much more research of this type to understand the role that particular tasks and guidance play in supporting students in developing new ways of thinking and knowing when to use them. Using a microgenetic approach, "the more precise the understanding that we can gain of any set of changes, the better our chance of theoretical progress in identifying [underlying] commonalities and thus of understanding long-term, as well as short- and medium-term changes" (Siegler & Crowley, 1991, p. 607). Such theoretical progress is needed if we are to understand how to sustain the short-term changes seen in such investigations over time and promote the production of lasting modifications of children's conceptual frameworks.

Despite arguing that the conceptual change that occurred during these DSAs in electricity provided substantial insights toward understanding the issue of developing scientific knowledge of electricity, we consider the amount of change to be a conservative estimate of how children of this age group may change with respect to the development of scientific knowledge of electricity. Whereas it is theoretically consistent with this approach to provide guidance with respect to scientific ideas as well as scientific reasoning, we generally provided guidance only with respect to scientific reasoning, and that guidance was minimal. Moreover, not every potential ZPD was formed or fully developed, as was noted in our previous discussion. With the knowledge that we have gained from this inquiry, we are now much more prepared to conduct interviews of this type and engage students in productive "zones;" hence, these findings should be considered as a first step toward understanding conceptual change in electricity. In addition, our findings that indicated a relation between the accuracy of conceptions of current and resistance suggest that more studies are needed to understand the *interrelations* among students' conceptions of important concepts in the topic area of electricity. Studies of students' conceptions of current have dominated the literature, and it is not uncommon in other topic areas to find that studies have focused on a single scientific concept in isolation, rather than examining the interrelations among concepts. Such studies are limited in helping us understand conceptual change and how to assist students in building integrated knowledge.

Finally, we suggest that these results indicate that we must remain open minded about the nature and occurrence of conceptual change. Hashweh (1986) pointed out that many studies of science learning, which have concluded that students' ideas are resistant to change, have often done so without establishing that an attempt was made to facilitate change or that the attempt was well-suited to promoting change. Constructs such as conceptual profile, which we find quite compelling in the re-presentation of conceptual change that it supports, may require many science educators to reconstruct beliefs about the nature of knowledge and learning to be embraced. Driver and Erickson (1983) called attention to this issue in arguing that adopting a constructivist view of knowledge acquisition required rejecting a rational–empirical view. This may be a daunting task for many science educators as evidenced by the observation 10 years later that a rational–empirical view continues to dominate the science conceptual change literature (J. P. Smith et al., 1993). Such a view of knowledge, which values a correspondence theory of truth, when applied to studies of learning, pays little attention to important aspects such as motivational processes (Pintrich, Marx, & Boyle, 1993; Strike & Posner, 1992). We do not know in many cases, for example, whether the students in such studies were intent on understanding the subject matter, and we do not know if they even shared the same understanding of the purpose of the tasks used to assess their understanding (e.g., Ames & Ames, 1989; Newman et al., 1989). Without this broader view of learning, we cannot discern whether any "resistance to change" has its source in the construction of the concept under study, or if it lies in some other aspect of the learning task.

It seems clear that the context in this study was one of student and other participant sharing a common perspective of the task at hand, which was to explain a part of the physical world. In the context of having their ideas valued, we saw a variety of creative and powerful ideas exhibited by the children. Were they scientifically accurate with respect to electricity? Not necessarily; however, we see the true value of scientific knowledge not its existence as formal, general, logical statements, but in its viability and its use. Taking a "snapshot" of what children know does little to illustrate their scientific understanding of the world as vital and dynamic, as something of use. Having children put their knowledge to use and allowing them to modify and develop their beliefs brings us closer to understanding conceptual change at a level from which we can comprehend knowledge construction on a developmental time frame. We believe that the approach we have described, DSA, is one tool that is likely to provide such insights about conceptual change in science.

REFERENCES

Ames, C., & Ames, R. (Eds.). (1989). *Research on motivation in education: Goals and cognitions.* San Diego: Academic.

Anderson, J. R. (1983). *The architecture of cognition.* Cambridge, MA: Harvard University Press.

Arnold, M., & Millar, R. (1987). Being constructive: An alternative approach to the teaching of introductory ideas in electricity. *International Journal of Science Education, 9,* 553–563.

Bachelard, G. (1968). *The philosophy of no* (G. C. Waterson, Trans.). New York: Orion. (Original work published 1940)

Brown, J. S., Collins, A., & Duguid, P. (1989). Situated cognition and the culture of learning. *Educational Researcher, 18,* 32–42.

Cazden, C. B. (1981). Performance before competence: Assistance to child discourse in the zone of proximal development. *The Quarterly Newsletter of the Laboratory of Comparative Human Cognition, 3*(1), 5–8.

Champagne, A. B., Gunstone, R. F., & Klopfer, L. E. (1985). Effecting changes in cognitive structures among physics students. In A. L. Pines (Ed.), *Cognitive structure and conceptual change* (pp. 163–187). Orlando, FL: Academic.

Champagne, A. B., Klopfer, L. E., & Anderson, J. H. (1980). Factors influencing the learning of classical mechanics. *American Journal of Physics, 48,* 1074–1079.

Chi, M. T. H. (1991). Conceptual change within and across ontological categories: Examples from learning and discovery in science. In R. Giere (Ed.), *Cognitive models of science: Minnesota studies in the philosophy of science* (pp. 129–186). Minneapolis: University of Minnesota Press.

Chi, M. T. H., Feltovich, P. J., & Glaser, R. (1981). Categorization and representation of physics problems by experts and novices. *Cognitive Science, 5,* 121–152.

Clement, J., Brown, D. E., & Zietsman, A. (1989). Not all preconceptions are misconceptions: Finding "anchoring conceptions" for grounding instruction on students' intuitions. *International Journal of Science Education, 11,* 554–565.

Confrey, J. (1990). A review of the research on student conceptions in mathematics, science, and programming. In C. Cazden (Ed.), *Review of research in education* (pp. 3–56). Washington, DC: American Educational Research Association.

diSessa, A. A. (1988). Knowledge in pieces. In G. Forman & P. Pufall (Eds.), *Constructivism in the computer age* (pp. 49–70). Hillsdale, NJ: Lawrence Erlbaum Associates, Inc.

Driver, R., Asoko, H., Leach, J., Mortimer, E., & Scott, P. (1994). Constructing scientific knowledge in the classroom. *Educational Researcher, 23*(7), 5–12.

Driver, R., & Easley, J. (1978). Pupils and paradigms: A review of the literature related to concept development in adolescent science students. *Studies in Science Education, 5,* 61–84.

Driver, R., & Erickson, G. (1983). Theories-in-action: Some theoretical and empirical issues in the study of students' conceptual frameworks in science. *Studies in Science Education, 10,* 37–60.

Einstein, A. (1950). *Out of my later years.* New York: Philosophical Library.

Gauld, C. F. (1988). The cognitive context of pupils' alternative frameworks. *International Journal of Science Education, 10,* 267–274.

Gilbert, J. K., & Watts, D. M. (1983). Concepts, misconceptions and alternative conceptions: Changing perspectives in science education. *Studies in Science Education, 10,* 61–98.

Glasersfeld, E. V. (1984). An introduction to radical constructivism. In P. Watzlawick (Ed.), *The invented reality* (pp. 17–40). New York: Norton.

Hashweh, M. Z. (1986). Toward an explanation of conceptual change. *European Journal of Science Education, 8,* 229–249.

Lave, J. (1988). *Cognition in practice: Mind, mathematics, and culture in everyday life.* Cambridge, England: Cambridge University Press.

Lewis, E. L., & Linn, M. C. (in press). Heat energy and temperature concepts of adolescents, naïve adults, and experts: Implications for curricular improvements. *Journal of Research in Science Teaching.*

Magnusson, S. J. (in press). Complexities of using computer-based tools: A case of inquiry about sound and music in the elementary school. *Journal of Science Education and Technology.*

Magnusson, S. J., Karr, C., George, A., & Boyle, R. A. (1994, March). *Multidisciplinary possibilities in project-based learning: Electricity and architecture.* Paper presented at the annual meeting of the National Science Teachers Association, Anaheim, CA.

Magnusson, S. J., & Palincsar, A. S. (in press). "We didn't try one with no water, so we don't know": Fourth graders' investigations of sound and music. *Science Education.*

McCloskey, M. (1983). Naive theories of motion. In D. Gentner & A. L. Stevens (Eds.), *Mental models* (pp. 299–323). Hillsdale, NJ: Lawrence Erlbaum Associates, Inc.

McDermott, L. C. (1984). Research on conceptual understanding in mechanics. *Physics Today, 37,* 24.

Metz, K. E. (1995). Reassessment of development constraints on children's science instruction. *Review of Educational Research, 65,* 93–127.

Mortimer, E. F. (1995). Conceptual change or conceptual profile change? *Science and Education, 4,* 267–285.

Newman, D., Griffin, P., & Cole, M. (1989). *The construction zone: Working for cognitive change in school.* Cambridge, MA: Cambridge University Press.

Osborne, R. (1983). Towards modifying children's ideas about electric current. *Research in Science & Technological Education, 1*(1), 73–82.

Osborne, R. J., & Gilbert, J. K. (1980). A method for the investigation of concept understanding in science. *European Journal of Science Education, 2,* 311–321.

Palincsar, A. S., Brown, A. L., & Campione, J. C. (1991). Dynamic assessment. In H. L. Swanson (Ed.), *Handbook on the assessment of learning disabilities: Theory, research, and practice* (pp. 75–94). Austin, TX: PRO-ED.

Piattelli-Palmarini, M. (1980). *Language and learning: The debate between Jean Piaget and Noam Chomsky.* London: Routledge & Kegan Paul.

Pintrich, P. R., Marx, R. W., & Boyle, R. (1993). Beyond "cold" conceptual change: The role of motivational beliefs and classroom contextual factors in the process of conceptual change. *Review of Educational Research, 63,* 167–199.

Posner, G. J., Strike, K. A., Hewson, P. W., & Gertzog, W. A. (1982). Accommodation of a scientific conception: Toward a theory of conceptual change. *Science Education, 66,* 211–227.

Reiner, M., Chi, M. T. H., & Resnick, L. (1988). Naive materialistic belief: An underlying epistemological commitment. In *Proceedings of the Tenth Annual Conference of the Cognitive Science Society* (pp. 544–551). Hillsdale, NJ: Lawrence Erlbaum Associates, Inc.

Russell, T. J. (1980). Children's understanding of simple electrical circuits. In T. J. Russell & A. P. C. Sia (Eds.), *Science and mathematics concept learning of South East Asian children: Second report on Phase II* (pp. 67–91). Glugar, Malaysia: SEAMEO-RECSAM.

Siegler, R. S., & Crowley, K. (1991). The microgenetic method: A direct means for studying cognitive development. *American Psychologist, 46,* 606–620.

Shipstone, D. (1985). Electricity in simple circuits. In R. Driver, E. Guesne, & A. Tiberghien (Eds.), *Children's ideas in science* (pp. 33–51). London: Milton Keynes.

Smagorinsky, P. (1995). The social construction of data: Methodological problems of investigating learning in the zone of proximal development. *Review of Educational Research, 65,* 191–212.

Smith, E. E., & Medin, D. L. (1981). *Categories and concepts.* Cambridge, MA: Harvard University Press.

Smith, J. P., diSessa, A. A., & Roschelle, J. (1993). Misconceptions reconceived: A constructivist analysis of knowledge in transition. *The Journal of the Learning Sciences, 3,* 115–163.

Solomon, J. (1983). Learning about energy: How pupils think in two domains. *European Journal of Science Education, 51,* 49–59.

Strike, K. A., & Posner, G. J. (1992). A revisionist theory of conceptual change. In R. A. Duschl & R. J. Hamilton (Eds.), *Philosophy of science, cognitive psychology, and educational theory and practice* (pp. 147–176). Albany: State University of New York Press.

Suppe, F. (1977). *The structure of scientific theories* (2nd ed.). Champagne–Urbana: University of Illinois Press.

Vygotsky, L. S. (1978). *Mind in society: The development of higher psychological processes* (M. Cole, V. John-Steiner, S. Scribner, & E. Souberman, Eds.). Cambridge, MA: Harvard University Press.

Wandersee, J. H., Mintzes, J. J., & Novak, J. D. (1994). Research on alternative conceptions in science. In D. Gabel (Ed.), *Handbook of research on science teaching and learning* (pp. 177–210). New York: Macmillan.

White, B. Y. (1993). Intermediate causal models: A missing link for successful science education? In R. Glaser (Ed.), *Advances in instructional psychology* (Vol. 4, pp. 177–252). Hillsdale, NJ: Lawrence Erlbaum Associates, Inc.